STORIES OF DISCIPLESHIP AND DEVOTIONAL LIFE

SCOTT R. WARD, DMin

AdventSource

Following Jesus
Stories of Discipleship and Devotional Life

Author: Scott R. Ward, DMin

Cover design and layout: Ramsey Mesnard

Additional copies of this resource are available from:
Advent*Source*
5120 Prescott Avenue
Lincoln, Nebraska 68506
AdventSource.org
402.486.8800

Copyright © 2023 by the North American Division Corporation of Seventh-day Adventists.

All rights reserved. No part of this publication may be reproduced, stored in a retrieval system, or transmitted, in any form or by any means, electronic, mechanical, photocopying, recording, or otherwise, without the prior written permission of the copyright holder.

Printed in the United States of America

ISBN# 978-1-57756-233-7

Acknowledgements

I would like to thank my students for inspiring me with their stories of discipleship and devotional life. As I read their essays, I knew their stories needed to be shared so others could be inspired as well. It seems discipleship is often cognitively understood as equipping for ministry but when challenged to look deeper into the heart by asking, "who?", we all begin to discover those who have nurtured our spirituality along the way from our earliest years.

A special thanks also to the many teachers, pastors, and parents who have discipled me over the years—I have been blessed to be nurtured by so many of you that it would be impossible to try naming you all. Currently, my closest discipler is my wife, Sarah. Sarah, thank you for praying with me, sharing devotional thoughts with me, challenging me when needed, and for creating a wonderfully nurturing home where spirituality is infused in all we do.

I would also like to thank my friends and co-workers who read through the rough draft of this book, giving great feedback and writing endorsements to encourage others to read as well. Finally, I'd like to thank my research assistant, Nancy Meszaros/Kardos-Moldovan . Nancy has spent many hours editing and tracking down information from students, working diligently to make this book what it is today. Her experience as an Academy Bible teacher has proved invaluable to this project.

In the end, all the glory goes to God for inspiring us to be disciples and to disciple others through Jesus' example and through the gift of the Holy Spirit. May this all be for his name's honor and glory, Amen.

Endorsements

"Dr. Ward writes in an authentic and practical style that puts the reader at ease like we've just sat down in a conversation together. It is an easy read, packed full of practical examples that teachers and principals can immediately apply. But more deeply, the transparency found within the plethora of rich stories feels like rare and honest insights that remind us of how human we are. In leadership, we so often fall into the trap of placing each other into quick categories or only seeing each other as our titles. This quick read takes us back to the humanness of who we are. What I appreciate most are the psychosocial developmental stages for adolescents that Dr. Ward applies to discipleship. He brilliantly demonstrates the necessity for creating your ministry within a youth's need for autonomy, identity, belonging, and purpose."

– *Angela White (Superintendent of School Growth, Oregon Conference of Seventh-day Adventists)*

"Dr. Scott Ward shares principles and experiences that will inspire you. The testimonies contained in this book will empower you as you consider your ministry calling and practices."

– *Dr. Tracy Wood (Youth & Young Adult Ministries Director, North American Division of Seventh-day Adventists)*

"During my engagement with Dr. Scott Ward in an After School Program amid the Covid-19 period, I observed his profound dedication to fostering a profound and affectionate connection between children and Jesus Christ.

This book presents a pragmatic approach, serving as a valuable resource for parents seeking to enhance their children's relationship with Christ. Furthermore, it extends an invigorating call to pastors, teachers, and mentors, encouraging collaborative efforts to deliberate on the discipleship journey within their respective church and school settings and to evaluate its impact on the students and families under their influence."

– *Pastor Claval Hunter (Associate Director for the Center for Community Change, Andrews University Theological Seminary of Seventh-day Adventists)*

"I recommend this book to anyone raising or working with kids, as it presents a refreshingly practical approach to discipleship. I appreciate the stories woven throughout this book that not only illustrate discipleship principles, but also communicate that a relationship is at the heart of discipleship. As a parent this book gives the opportunity to be more intentional, what is working and what could be changed to better disciple our children? Take your time as you read through the chapters, fully engage in the activities, and embrace the discipleship journey that God is calling you on."

– *Ben Martin (Pastor of Children and Family Discipleship, Pioneer Memorial Church)*

"As an academy teacher who has collaborated between school, church, and home, I believe this book prepares us with the tools - both spiritually and organizationally - to create a foundation of discipleship, support, and love for the younger generation(s). Dr. Ward provides valuable steps for personal spiritual development and discipleship which I can use in my school setting with my students. I am pleased to say that this book aims at a united ministry between these three spheres of influence, all while showcasing real examples of this collaboration and discipleship through stories. While it is a must read for everyone, I hope this book becomes a treasured staple for every teacher."

– Nancy Meszaros/Kardos-Moldovan (Religion/Bible Teacher, Andrews Academy)

"We often seek to systematize discipleship into a program so we can 'make more disciples' in less time. But what if God never intended it to be that way? Scott Ward has recaptured the essence of discipleship as a personal journey with God that can be encouraged and explored as each individual deepens their walk by actually utilizing the very tools God has built into them. This book actually helped me discover a few more ways that I could 'be still and know' as I continue on my own journey."

– Don Keele, Jr. (Director of Young Adult Ministry and Adventist Christian Fellowship, Georgia-Cumberland Conference)

Contents

Foreword i

Preface v

Introduction vii

Part 1 xvii

    Ch 1: The Discipleship Process According to John 1 1

    Ch 2: Who Discipled You: Stories from My Students.... 15

    Ch 3: Telling Our Stories to the Next Generation 35

    Ch 4: Finding Your Story Through Three 47

    Ch 5: Why Campus-Based Ministry is Important in Forming Worldview 57

Part 2 71

    Ch 6: My Story and Devotional Life.............................. 75

    Ch 7: Stories of Devotional Lives and Styles 87

    Ch 8: Sarah's Story and Devotional Life 125

Part 3 137

Ch 9: Elementary (K-8) Church School Discipleship Action Plan 141

Ch 10: Academy (9-12) Discipleship Action Plan 155

Ch 11: Public School Discipleship Action Plan............ 173

Ch 12: Helping Live Your Story to the Fullest 191

Appendices... 197

Foreword

I have known Scott Ward for many years—first as one of my students in a doctoral Biblical Spirituality class and now, more recently, as a friend and colleague. Each fall we both teach sections of a required seminary course on the basics of Biblical Spirituality. I especially enjoy the joint spiritual retreats we have for all our students together at the beginning of the semester where we get to walk and talk and pray with each other and be together with our students for an entire day. I believe what he has written here will be an explanation on what we do to help our students know and love Jesus more intimately. Our students always tell us how much they have been blessed by the retreat, prayer walks, and the practices outlined in this book, and I know you too will be blessed as well.

In this book, *Following Jesus: Stories of Discipleship and Devotional Life,* Scott does an outstanding job helping us understand what discipleship is and how it works. Taking his cue from Jesus who taught biblical values and theology through stories, he illustrates the concepts of discipleship and devotional life by telling heartwarming stories from his life and the lives of many of his students. There is a variety of stories showing how discipleship can take place in multiple ways and under different circumstances in natural settings. Ultimately, discipleship is about someone loving another person and taking the time to invest his or her life in that individual. The genius of this book is that discipleship is not a program or complicated lifestyle, it is living out the Christian life with love and intentionally and passing it on to the next generation.

I loved reading his biblical insight on discipleship based on John chapter 1. There is much to learn and apply as we commit ourselves to grow in Jesus and help others do the same.

Here is the basic discipleship process as Scott sees it in John 1:

1. Dissatisfaction with life and seeking something better.
2. Listening to the testimonies of others for answers and a better life.
3. Looking for consistency, authenticity, and meaning: Watching to see if the actions of others match the testimonies.
4. Challenging them to try what others say and do.
5. Committing and engaging in community if they see that it works and makes a difference.
6. The result is a call to care and share what has happened.

This chapter lays the ground for the rest of the book by illustrating these concepts thorough many testimonies. Scott also gives us the tools to do the same in our own context.

Pastors, teachers, and parents will find many helpful tips on how to share their faith and values with the new generation. Scott really captures the instruction outlined in Deuteronomy 6, the Shema, of how to seize every opportunity of how parents, teachers, and pastors can disciple their children.

If parents, teachers, and concerned church members are serious about passing on the torch of faith to the next generation, this book is a must read—I enjoyed reading it and received a rich blessing from its many concepts and stories, and I know you will too. And just as I look forward to continued prayer walks and conversations "along the way" with friends, colleagues, and with my students, I pray that what is written in these pages will help you be inspired and equipped to have more conversations about spiritual matters and share many testimonies with the fellow travelers that you meet along life's way.

—S. Joseph Kidder, DMin

Professor of Discipleship and Applied Theology, SDATS, Andrews University

Author of: "Journey to the Heart of God," "The Big 4," "Living With the Mind of Jesus," "Moving Your Church," "Majesty," and "Out of Babylon."

Preface

I have just spent one week teaching an intensive class on Foundations of Biblical Spirituality to a group of pastors. Some came in burned out and feeling like they were on the brink of quitting, but we all left our week together feeling encouraged by the Holy Spirit and having found some new friends.

Pastors aren't the only ones; I know there are teachers and parents who feel this way sometimes and need encouragement too. This book on discipleship is not to give you one more task or another method of how to do your work. Hopefully it will be an inspiration to live life in ministry just a bit differently, whether it's pastoral ministry or teaching ministry or ministry in the home. I have found that if we can connect our hearts to God more fully, and be discipled by him on a daily basis, we can allow that nurturing relationship to freely flow to those within our sphere of influence, discipling them to Jesus as well. As Jesus disciples us, we pass that along and disciple others. And when we see the fruits of our labor growing in those we disciple, it encourages us and lifts our spirits, giving us hope and carrying us forward. This is how Jesus intended ministry to be, as we work through the sustaining power of the Holy Spirit. And this, for me, is what puts the joy into the journey of ministering to others as both a pastor and a teacher.

What you will find in the pages ahead is all about relationships and all about stories. It includes many stories from my students sharing testimonies of who discipled them so you can see examples from a wide variety of people from around the world. It also includes stories of individuals' devotional lives so you can see some examples and ideas and be inspired that some of those same things may work for you.

So take heart and read on, praying for the Holy Spirit to inspire you along the way and to guide you in your search for deeper meaning and purpose in your spirituality and in your mission to those you serve. I pray that one of the results of you spending time in this book will be to have a closer walk with Jesus, and a closer walk with your fellow pastors, teachers, and parents as you learn how to better disciple each other as you disciple the younger generations which surround you as well.

The Shema

[4] "Listen, O Israel! The Lord is our God, the Lord alone. [5] And you must love the Lord your God with all your heart, all your soul, and all your strength. [6] And you must commit yourselves wholeheartedly to these commands that I am giving you today. [7] Repeat them again and again to your children. Talk about them when you are at home and when you are on the road, when you are going to bed and when you are getting up. [8] Tie them to your hands and wear them on your forehead as reminders. [9] Write them on the doorposts of your house and on your gates.

Introduction

It seems to me that a lot of what has been written about discipleship is for those who attend church regularly. But can discipleship be for the outliers? For those who are struggling in the messiness of life and losing their way every other day? Can discipleship be evangelistic? Reaching to the margins? Can it be for all the young people who we see not only in our homes, churches, and schools, but also in the community?

Too often we assume that the children born into our own homes are Christian, but they are not. Not yet. I believe one of the biggest mistakes is not taking the time to disciple our own children according to the ancient tradition of the Shema. The Israelites knew it, but many Christians have somehow forgotten. Rabbi Jonathan Sacks in his book, "Lessons in Leadership," states:

> "So Jews became the only people in history to predicate their very survival on education. The most sacred duty of parents was to teach their children. Passover itself became an ongoing seminar in the handing on of memory. Judaism became the religion whose heroes were teachers and whose passion was study and the life of the mind The Mesopotamians built ziggurats. The Egyptians built pyramids. The Greeks built the Parthenon. The Romans built the Coliseum. Jews built schools. That is why they alone, of all the civilizations of the ancient world, are still

alive and strong, still continuing their ancestors' vocation, their heritage intact and undiminished."[1]

Schools were the way the Jews discipled young people while they were "on the road" throughout the day. The goal of this book is to lay out ideas which can be helpful in getting back to that model and discipling the young people born into Adventist homes, as well as those born into homes in the communities around our churches and church schools.

The target audience for this book is pastors, teachers, and parents. The main approach I am advocating is campus-based ministry—especially where parents, pastors, and teachers have the opportunity to co-minister to young people, either in Adventist church school or on public campuses—and the discipleship principles which can be applied to other contexts as well. One such example is the story Kalisa shares about how discipleship shaped her to be the person she is today:

KALISA

My church family, the local pastors, and my parents had made a large enough impression on me that I wanted to be like them. Therefore, my parents dropped me off at the office of a chaplain named Dilys. From eighth grade through twelfth grade, I watched her engage with students who would come by and find her. She would sit them down and pour into them, allowing me to see her personal conversations with students and faculty members. As I sat there over the years, I noticed a pattern. She was

---

[1] Sacks, Jonathan. "Lessons in Leadership". (2015) Maggid Books An imprint of Koren Publishers Jerusalem Ltd. POB 8531, New Milford, CT 06776-8531, USA & POB 4044, Jerusalem 9104001, Israel, p. 74
Also in: https://www.santafejcc.com/parshah/article_cdo/aid/2430669/jewish/The-Far-Horizon.htm#utm_source=domain&utm_medium=domain&utm_campaign=chabadsantafe

always genuine in how she spoke. She would look at the student(s), engaged. She would ask questions that made one ponder what they thought or felt about their situation. Most importantly, she was always talking about this Middle Eastern rabbi, Jesus, like he was someone she really truly believed in and had a relationship with.

When she wasn't engaging with students, she would ask me questions about my own life: what I thought about God, ministry, and my emotions, how I would evaluate my life currently with Jesus, why I evaluated my life that way, and she would give me books to read to learn more about Jesus and myself.

When I left for college, she kept tabs on me, and when I came back for breaks, she opened her home for me to visit anytime. She had a community that met at her home every Tuesday and she invited me to join. I was able to create an adult community with doctors and Ph.D. students, and engage with them in how they live adult life and do Christianity. I was able to become close to her family, which in turn, put me in position to do my first pastoral internship at her husband's church and meet a new community. While I was figuring out how to be a Christian without my parents, her home gave me a safe community to evaluate what I had been doing each semester and encourage me to try again.

I have the most profound respect for the woman who discipled me, and I have also seen my theology of God change because of the love she has shown me. When people ask me the story of Jesus, I get teary-eyed, because this is true: Jesus' love is precious to me. When I tell people about Jesus, I always tell them about a God who has stuck by my side and moved me into his family, because that is what has been discipled to me.

Multiple studies conducted over the past decade or two within Christianity (including Adventism) show that we are losing more and more of our children from attending and being involved in church.[2] Perhaps we could say the problem began when we raised our kids in a Christian environment but failed to effectively introduce them to ways of developing their own relationships with Jesus. Growing that deep, personal relationship is the only way of being authentically tied to the church in the healthiest way.[3] Thus, the goal here is to look closely at what discipleship really is and to chart a course that will help us get on track with reaching our own children for Jesus.

In Chapter 1, we will lay the foundation for this book by looking at a discipleship process based on the writings of the apostle John. I love anything and everything that was written by John, who was a son of thunder, the youngest and most intimate disciple of Jesus, the great lover of souls, the disciple who couldn't be martyred, and the prophet of Patmos.

I love how he talks to us—even today—as little children.

I love how he chose to record Jesus telling us to love one another and included the beautiful prayer Jesus offered for each of us in John 17.

I love how he decides to include the parable about the intimate connection of the vine and the branches and the fruit that can flow from that relationship.

---

[2] Dudley, Roger L. "Youth Religious Commitment over Time: A Longitudinal Study of Retention." Review of Religious Research, vol. 41, no. 1, Oct. 1999, pp. 110–21.

[3] Jiménez, Obed. "The Relationship Between Parental Influence and Christian Spiritual Practices Among Adventist Youth in Puerto Rico." Dissertations, Digital Commons @ Andrews University, 2009.

I love how he silently underscores the miracles when Jesus never physically touched anyone, to reassure us that our physical separation from Jesus today doesn't hinder our lives from being touched by him we can still be in an intimate relationship with him every day.[4]

I also love how John—unlike the other gospel writers—chose to include the story about Jesus, after his resurrection, asking Peter three times, "Do you love Me?"

I learn a great deal about God from the entire body of scripture, but my heart is the most deeply touched by this book from John. Within his writings, I have found a discipleship process that not only helps me find my own personal relationship with Jesus but also demonstrates how to most effectively share that with the world around me. I believe John's great focus on becoming a loving gospel testimony for the world around us is even more relevant today than ever before: he paired discipleship and evangelism.

I don't believe in the separation of discipleship and evangelism.[5] The 72 disciples whom Jesus sent out to do ministry in Luke 10, were sent before their relationship with Jesus was well refined. They were called to go and share, as they were, so they could understand and draw closer to him. To understand this properly, we must understand what evangelism really is. I would like to offer that evangelism is simply sharing our testimony of what Jesus has done and is doing for us on a daily basis. This is gospel evangelism in its truest form. We have scriptural examples of this with the woman at the well and the demoniac who was freed from oppression. After being accepted, loved, and freed, they

---

[4] Idea borrowed from Dr. John Paulien, in his Bible Amplifier book on the gospel of John.

[5] Discipleship and evangelism together. This is not common in many discipleship models, but in youth ministry, it is rather common to keep the two together. The D6 model, etc.

immediately went and shared their testimony with others—they were so full of gratitude and joy they couldn't help but share what Jesus had done.

This is the relationship theology that has always driven my campus-based ministries with children, youth, and young adults. It's about living out the Shema, hearing and obeying, and taking appropriate action every day. Discipleship doesn't work as a weekend-only event; it can only work if it's the daily norm. Without access to our kids throughout the week, we just don't have the opportunity to fully engage in this type of discipling and leading our children to Jesus.

The reality of the statistics is that leaving discipleship up to the parents alone isn't working because so many parents have not been discipled themselves. Even in Jesus' day, it took a village to raise and nurture the children and youth, and ideally, today we all need a spiritual community helping each other by doing our best to help each other follow Jesus.[6]

Chapter 2 is a collection of stories from my seminary students which answers the question, "Who discipled you?" You have just read one of these discipleship stories, and there are many more in store within this chapter. These stories are from around the world and illustrate some of the vast diversity of culture and experience represented here at Andrews University—one of the most diverse campuses in the world. My prayer is that in these stories you'll find inspiration and examples for identifying your own story of discipleship and how you can pass that on by seeing new and fresh ways to disciple within your sphere of influence.

In Chapter 3, we will look at the power of story. People across the world and throughout time have passed on their values, beliefs, and love by telling stories. The Shema, Jesus'

---

[6] Beagles, Kathleen. "Growing Disciples in Community." Christian Education Journal, vol. 9, no. 1, Spring 2012, pp. 148–64.

parables, the vine and the branches, and the many lessons learned by observing sheep serve as examples of discipleship that centers on inviting others into the shared story of the group. It's an invitation to belong, take part, contribute, and take ownership of an important role in the community.

Community and church roles vary greatly depending on talents, interests, and needs. True heartfelt belonging will never be experienced by those coming in if they don't find that place of meaning and contribution. All too often, if this belonging aspect of the church experience is missing, many will likely leave. It is vitally important each person sees how the story of their life fits into the story of Jesus and his mission to the world.

In Chapter 4, we look at the Three-Story approach to sharing worship thoughts. I was introduced to this concept by Steve Case many years ago in the Connecting seminars he conducted to help youth pastors in Northern California teach youth how to share worship talks. This is still a powerful tool for connecting with youth—sharing funny stories and matching the moral of that story to the moral of a Bible story, telling them one after the other, and then helping your audience to make application to their own lives. It may sound slightly complicated here but after you finish the chapter, I'm sure you'll be excited to give it a try!

In Chapter 5, we will discuss the importance of campus-based youth ministry. If we don't have access to our children during the week, it is very hard to teach them the ways of the Lord according to the great tradition of the Shema. If our children only experience church and Christian community on the weekends, we must ask ourselves what influences are informing our children's worldviews the other five days per week (hint: that device in their pockets is one of the most powerful influences in their lives and it's discipling them to rival God's).

First, we will look at maximizing the potential of having our children attend church schools to make sure true discipleship goes beyond mentoring and is happening there and then. We will discuss some options for supporting our children who do not have access to Christian education. We will also discuss how to help our children make sense of the worldview presented to them in non-Christian schools, and how to do our best to bring a Christian worldview into whatever setting our children may find themselves now and in the future, whether it be a public school or a secular workplace after graduation.

In Chapters 6-8, we will take a look at devotional life as the core of Christianity and the primary foundation for discipleship. In these chapters, we will be revisiting and renewing concepts of commitment to Jesus and devotional practices I first laid out in my book, "Authentic: Where True, Life-Changing Christianity Begins" (R&H 2012). I believe the ultimate goal of raising our young people is to help them go beyond admiring the devotional lives of others to developing their own life-changing relationships with Jesus. This personal connection, in my experience, is the truest way to living lives of meaning and purpose filled with all the fruits of the Spirit.

One of the biggest challenges of being a spiritual leader and influencer in the lives of children is for pastors, teachers, and parents to do their best to live and model this as much as possible for them. For inspiration on this challenging topic, I will be sharing some details of who I am as a person—hobbies, interests, talents, and temperament. All of these things impact how I personally nurture my relationship with Jesus. I have also asked others to share who they are and how that impacts how they relate to God. Hopefully this will help each reader to find the ways they can best nurture their personal relationship with Jesus, which will then impact how they disciple others.

In Chapters 9 and 10 I want to take some time to look at action plans for creating a well-rounded and balanced approach for interaction with children within a K-12 church school setting. It is important to understand that devotional time with an 8-year-old will look different than devotional time with an 18-year-old. In my experience, there are many teachers, pastors, and parents who make efforts toward leading young people spiritually but become frustrated because they feel they are not connecting well nor being effective through the same approaches they use for themselves or perhaps with other adults. In these chapters, I will present key elements I believe help form intentional discipleship experiences: bonding, teaching doctrine, teaching devotional life, outreach, evangelism, and worship.

In Chapter 11, I will take some time to look at action plans for creating a well-rounded and balanced approach for discipling children in settings *other* than church schools. This will include the public high school setting, and we will look at the potential for developing Christian preschools and after-school tutoring programs to reach urban populations and other communities where finances and other resources can be a challenge.

Finally, Chapter 12 is the wrap-up and send-off for the entire book so you can start trying out what you've learned here and discipling the young people within your sphere of influence.

The overall goal of this book is to find as many ways as we can to raise all God's children so they can experience for themselves how wide, how long, how deep, and how high God's love really is for each of them. In Ephesians 3, Paul talks about this experience of loving and being loved by God as not reserved for God's chosen people alone, but for everyone, no matter what home, culture, environment, or situation they were born into. The mission of the first angel of Revelation 14 is to take the Gospel to every tribe, tongue, nation, and people—to give everyone, everywhere the best chance possible for knowing Jesus and becoming his disciples. This is also known as the great gospel commission laid out in the four gospels. If we can learn to share this most important message more effectively with our own children, perhaps this will help us be more effective in sharing the gospel with those outside our own homes and churches as well.

Part 1
Understanding the Critical Importance of Discipling Young People

Discipleship involves relationship. Merely giving information rarely changes people and we can only be heard at the deepest levels of the heart when we first show that we care. President Theodore Roosevelt is famously quoted as saying, "No one cares how much you know until they know how much you care." This is still true today—especially in discipling young people.

As a youth pastor and teacher, I found that it was critically important to find ways to connect with young people outside of church and outside of the classroom to build relationships for my ministry to be effective. In the Blueprint film on Adventist Education one educator said, "There is no significant learning without a significant relationship with the teacher." Jesus modeled this throughout His time on earth and it is testified to by His own disciples. In 1 John 1 the apostle states that his goal is to share what he and his friends had, seen, heard and touched with their own eyes, ears and hands. And he says that it was through their relationships with Jesus that he and the other disciples knew that eternal life was only through Jesus! Stories told in the context of relationship can be some of the most powerful influences known to humankind, and transformative testimonies about the love of Jesus help to form a powerful context where discipleship can flourish.

Chapter 1

The Discipleship Process According to John 1

I was born into an Adventist home near Loma Linda, California, in the 1960s. At that time and place, there were so many Adventists living in such a concentrated area that, if I remember right, even the mail was delivered on Sunday instead of on the Sabbath! I remember thriving churches and overflowing church schools. I remember this new sensational singing group that appeared called the Heritage Singers. Those were the days!

I was, and still am, an introvert. I could, and still can, entertain myself for hours while getting lost in my own thoughts and dreams. My own imagination was better than anything TV or books had to offer when I was a kid. This was during the time when LEGOs came in only square and rectangular shapes and you had to make up your own creations. This I eagerly did: no directions, no plans, no one else creating for me. It was all up to each child to create and bring into existence their dreams.

After finishing second grade at the Loma Linda church school, my family moved to Minnesota, next door to my grandparents and back to where my dad had grown up. There we lived in the country rather than on a city block, and I had free roam of the farm. My grandfather had converted the land into Ward's Auto Sales, a used car and farm machinery business, back in 1949. He also sold parts from broken cars, tractors, and machinery. I lived my childhood dream on that land—exploring the swamp, herding cows, trapping pocket gophers, riding minibikes (child-sized motorcycles), and generally getting lost in the clouds of my thoughts and adventures every day. Dirt, mosquitos, wood ticks, cuts, and bruises were not a problem for me. I eagerly embraced them all!

My first year in Minnesota, there was no church school, so I attended public school in the 3rd grade. The teacher was nice, but for some reason I just felt out of place. Third grade is the first time I remember getting punched by another kid. By the time the next school year started, my little church had decided to open their own school for me and my older brother, and a family with four kids that had recently moved to town. This happened in the early 70s—at the peak of enrollment in Adventist church schools in North America.

I graduated from 8th grade at that little church school and ended up going to a public high school for a couple of years. I eventually left home to attend a boarding academy in Hutchinson, Minnesota, just a few hours south of where we lived. After graduating, I attended an Adventist college for three years before finishing my Bachelor of Fine Arts at the University of Nebraska.

I loved my years in church school, and I loved my church family, because I felt deeply they were my family. We did everything together: grade school, Sabbath School, summer camp, Pathfinders, sleepovers at each other's houses, potlucks and church picnics, Saturday night table games with loads of desserts. Genuine love and community surrounded me. What is astonishing to me is that despite this wonderful, accepting environment created by loving Christian parents and church leaders, I launched into college and still fell into the worldly party scene which welcomed me as a young adult. I was not rebellious or looking for trouble; I was that "good" kid that always did what he was told. But as an introvert, I simply went the way of the people who reached out and befriended me. In my situation, it wasn't the religious or spiritual people; it was the partiers.

I ran with that crowd for a few years until I became disgusted with myself and all that I was doing; and yet, there didn't seem to be anything in the church to catch my attention as meaningful or helpful to bring me back. So, one night after drinking and dancing at a local college bar, God told me, "You are coming with Me." He gave me a grand vision that I would be working for Him in some special way. And He began to open doors before me.

He led me into student colporteur work for a summer. I then led those programs for six years. Afterward, I attended seminary, and for 20 years I served as a youth and young adult pastor before being invited to move to Michigan to teach at the Seventh-day Adventist Theological Seminary on the campus of Andrews University.

As I have thought about my experiences over the years, it seems to me that the missing piece in my spiritual experience was that I wasn't introduced to a personal relationship with Jesus. I wasn't taught how to have meaningful devotional time. I was very well mentored and loved, but not discipled. I wasn't challenged to do outreach or to go on mission trips because those were not common things at the time. My church and church community did everything the denomination outlined at that time on how to raise children to know God. There was a lot of teaching "about" God, but very little about "knowing" God.

By the time I began attending Union College in Lincoln, Nebraska, we had a new pastor named Morris Venden who was preaching a revolutionary new message called "righteousness by faith," as opposed to righteousness by works. This was long before teaching discipleship became popular. In my experience, even today, I feel that Adventism still doesn't understand discipleship very well. That is the reason for this book: to create better opportunities for all our children to find what seemed to be missing from the church during my childhood—a culture that nurtures a personal and intimate experiential relationship with Jesus all day, every day.

This is my story. It's what I have, and it's shaped who I am. It's the background from which I approach scripture. My experience and temperament, have had a great impact on how I read the story of the calling of the first disciples, recorded in John 1. I hope the principles outlined in the following pages will be of help to anyone who is still searching for Jesus within their own story.

Because of my love for the writings of John, I find the discipleship model I relate to best is in chapter one of the gospel according to John. I'm sure there are other places for people with other personality types, learning styles, and love languages to find inspiration for reaching the world around them for Christ; this is simply the inspiration that makes sense to me as I journey through life. To condense things a bit, I'll pull out the verses I focus on in the calling-of-the-disciples story, keeping in mind the circumstances of Roman oppression which surrounded Israel and the people of Jesus' day at that time.

The First Disciples

> [6] God sent a man, John the Baptist,[c] [7] to tell about the light so that everyone might believe because of his testimony. [8] John himself was not

the light; he was simply a witness to tell about the light. ⁹ The one who is the true light, who gives light to everyone, was coming into the world.

³⁵ The following day John was again standing with two of his disciples. ³⁶ As Jesus walked by, John looked at him and declared, "Look! There is the Lamb of God!" ³⁷ When John's two disciples heard this, they followed Jesus.

³⁸ Jesus looked around and saw them following. "What do you want?" he asked them.

They replied, "Rabbi" (which means "Teacher"), "where are you staying?"

³⁹ "Come and see," he said. It was about four o'clock in the afternoon when they went with him to the place where he was staying, and they remained with him the rest of the day.

⁴⁰ Andrew, Simon Peter's brother, was one of these men who heard what John said and then followed Jesus. ⁴¹ Andrew went to find his brother, Simon, and told him, "We have found the Messiah" (which means "Christ"[a]).

As I have read, pondered, taught, and written on this passage within the context of my own story, I have put together a six-step "Discipleship Process" that emerged. It's not a prescriptive formula or program; it's not a "six weeks and done" event, it's what I hope can be a simple descriptive guideline to help those with a desire to disciple others—especially young people—for Jesus.

The first step I see in this passage, and in my own story, is a dissatisfaction with life. The people in Jesus' day were suffering under Roman oppression and looking for a way out. The religious leaders taught about the prophecy of a coming Messiah who would be a military leader to conquer the Romans and free God's people. People were listening to John the Baptist along with other preachers in hopes that this Messiah was near.

In my own story, there was a sort of dissatisfaction as well. When I drifted from church, I was in transition from high school to college, moving to a new city and a new school. At that time, Daniel and Revelation seminars were very popular, but I couldn't find relevance. I told myself I would rather spend my time getting to know Jesus rather than spending my time trying to figure out exactly when He was coming. My rationale was that if I knew Him, I would recognize Him when He showed up.

The problem was that the only thing I remember people saying about devotional life was to read the Bible and pray. Well, I had no idea what part of the Bible to read, or how to engage with what the verses said. I had followed a "read your Bible in a year" program and occasionally read my Sabbath School lessons, but that's about it. As far as my prayer experience, we would pray for missionaries, pastors, and teachers around the world, with a few other requests, but there was no mention of talking to Jesus as you would to a friend.

So my story of dissatisfaction with life was really a typical young adult journey to find my own faith. It was up to me to navigate the challenges of the world within my own Adventist worldview, and I didn't feel prepared for that. I was lost and had no practical ideas about how the Bible could guide me through life or help me make good choices. I floundered like I still see so many young people doing today.

The second step I see in this passage, and in my own life, was that in the floundering and searching, people of

Jesus' day (and mine) are listening to the testimonies of others whom they meet, and they try to find a good path to something better. In the story of John 1, we see how John the Baptist had faithful disciples who listened to many preachers but who had settled in as his followers. Maybe they liked that he didn't claim to be the Messiah himself, but that he would help them find Him? What we do know for sure is that John the Baptist had done such a good job at discipling that when he pointed out the Messiah, at least a few of his followers believed his testimony and immediately left him to follow Jesus.

In my story, I listened to the testimony of my peers who were going out to the bars, dancing, drinking, and doing everything else that typically goes with that lifestyle. I was invited into that community and gladly went because the people were so nice and welcoming. I just wanted a place of belonging, and this was the only option being offered. They made the party scene seem really appealing. And then, of course, all the beer commercials on TV painted an even more compelling picture of how popular you can be if you just drink Bud Light®! And what is baffling to me is that even as a good, rule-following, non-rebellious kid, I didn't see anything wrong with what I was doing. After all, "everyone was doing it"—even all my Adventist friends.

This leads us to step three in the discipleship process. After hearing the testimonies of those around me, and in Jesus' day the testimonies given by various leaders, we all looked at the lives of those sharing the testimonies. John's disciples obviously saw something in him that made them think his testimony was working for him. He seemed happy, fulfilled, and on a meaningful mission. That's what they were apparently searching for because that's what they eventually embraced as followers of Jesus. The people sharing their testimonies with me were good-looking and well-dressed, smiling, laughing, and talking about all the fun they were having, so why not try it?

This third point is a very important one as we think about how we are discipling young people today—do the religion and spirituality we proclaim actually make us happy and nice? Young people can see from a mile away if you practice what you preach and whether this makes you angry or happy. I think we've all met angry religious people who are not practicing what they expect others to, and most kids today won't have anything to do with this approach. (Let's be honest—most adults won't, either!)

This brings us to step number four. This is the point to which people have to get for them to be willing to try what you are inviting them to try. They typically need to be (1) searching for something new, then (2) listening to what you're promoting and (3) seeing if it actually makes you happy before (4) jumping in and trying it for themselves. I persistently kept trying the party life for almost three years. At first, it seemed really fun, but rather quickly I started feeling guilty about the things I was doing. I felt conflicted about hangovers and hookups, but everyone kept saying it was so great and fun. We all want to live a good life, right? And many times, it seems easier to pretend it really is good when it isn't, because then we would have to start the search all over again if we really haven't found The Good Life. The delusions and deceptions begin and continue until something extreme happens to shake us up and shake us out of whatever deception we are living in.

We see this regularly in the news—the Hollywood elites acting as though they have it all and are happy beyond belief, but for some reason are actually addicted to drugs and alcohol to cope with it all. Tragically, sometimes someone who appears to have it all takes their own life amidst the misery they can no longer endure. It's sad that this is reality for so many.

This all leads to step five. When we believe that this really does look like The Good Life, we commit to that lifestyle and to the community which supports it, oftentimes to the point of accepting deceptions as reality. For me and many others who have tried the ways of the world, we go from one worldly deception to another in search of the happiness which is promised but never fully received. There may be fun for a season, but the lasting joy never comes.

In the story of John 1, there is a better result for those who listened to John's advice and followed Jesus. They followed Him to "see where He was staying," and they found His life was consistent with His teachings. They found that when they left everything to be in community with Him, they experienced meaning, purpose, and joy. They found new identities in Him and in His mission.

This consistency between talk and walk leads to step six: they spontaneously go out and share what they have found with their friends. In John 1, the disciples go and tell everyone about the Messiah—not out of legalistic obligation, but out of uncontrollable joy at having found true meaning and purpose during troublesome times. This is the step I was missing in my own story – at least at first.

So, here is the basic discipleship process model as I see it:

1. **Context of Searching:** Dissatisfaction with life and seeking a sense of belonging

2. **Natural Curiosity:** Listening to the testimonies of others for answers

3. **Looking for Consistency, Authenticity, and Meaning:** Watching to see if actions match the testimonies

4. **Challenge to Try:** Trying what others say and do

5. **Commit to Community:** Engaging in community if it seems to be working

6. **Called to Care:** Spontaneously serving and sharing what has happened

Based on the model above, this is how I see my mission in life:

1. Learn to recognize those who are searching

2. Share my testimony openly

3. Do my best to live a Godly example consistent with what I claim to believe

4. Invite others to try what I believe in and provide opportunities for them to do so

5. Accept others into a welcoming and healing community that includes humanitarian and gospel outreach

6. Encourage others to become disciple-makers, sharing what has happened in their lives

The last step is to make application of this model to disciple children in our church schools and to lay that spiritual relational foundation in their lives which can see them through the troublesome times we all face. We will flesh this out in the school discipleship plan, but for now, this is the outline according to the model we are establishing here:

1. **Recognize students' struggles.** Erik Erickson's stages of psychosocial development and Kara Powell's research both identify that the primary task for adolescents is to be in search of autonomy, identity, belonging, and purpose.[1] This means that the primary tasks of the church during these years are to help

[1] McLeod, Saul. "Erik Erikson's stages of psychosocial development." (2013).; Powell, Kara, Jake Mulder, and Brad Griffin. "Growing young: Six essential strategies to help young people discover and love your church." Baker Books, 2016.

young people (1) find their identity in Christ, (2) belong within the church community, and (3) have a meaningful purpose with which to be engaged. If we fail to offer meaningful answers and opportunities to our children and youth, there are a plethora of others eagerly attempting to disciple our children by offering competing answers to this search.

2. **Teachers/parents/pastors share testimony according to the Shema, all day, every day, whether they realize it or not.** In order for adults within the sphere of influence on our children's lives to have a deep and meaningful spiritual impact on young people, they must have found a relationship with Jesus themselves. Young people are very forgiving and generous in recognizing that adults are not perfect, but they can also tell if the search is important to those who are in positions of influence in their lives. If young people don't sense a genuine and sincere search and testimony of faith at even a very basic level, they recognize that and will question its importance in their lives.

3. **Parents/pastors/teachers model faith and the fruits of the Spirit.** This is a part of number two as described above, by going beyond words and looking closely at actions. Students will be especially turned off to spirituality when they see a big disconnect between strong spiritual talk and a completely different lifestyle in one's personal life. Students can also see and greatly respect an adult who is uncontrollably overflowing with love and kindness. When the adults who have influence in the lives of our children are overflowing with grace and love, this is very compelling and attractive to young people—and everyone else!

4. **Mentoring/discipling relationships by pastors/teachers/parents.** When the fruits of the Spirit are flowing, young people are attracted to individuals demonstrating these fruits. This is a prime opportunity for those adults to offer "extra" conversations and time together with the young people who are craving positive spiritual influences in their lives.

5. **Parents/teachers/pastors create community with students.** As the relationship develops as described above, there is the opportunity to create a strong community young people can commit to, in which they can find belonging as their identity is formed and they find their personal mission. This step is by far the most involved and complex in the discipling process and can include a wide variety of elements such as: nurturing opportunities, social connection, counseling and help with deep personal issues, outreach opportunities, gospel evangelism, etc. This is where the community can become a strong village which nurtures and cares for its members with great intentionality. Ideally, this is also where we can see holistic care for body, mind, and spirit, and where we see collaboration between the church, church schools, Adventist Health, and other organizations which are a part of the broader Adventist network.

6. **Students will naturally share what impacts them.** When the first five steps above are positively impacting young people's lives, they will naturally share their love for their church and community, providing opportunities for spiritual growth like we see in Acts 2 and 3.

I have created a model to show this progression and details in a table chart format; all on one page:

A Discipleship Process Model	Jesus' Example	Worldly Discipleship	My Mission	My Church School
1. Dissatisfaction with life and seeking for something better	People in Jesus' day are suffering from Roman oppression and zealots and messiahs are everywhere	People are dissatisfied and searching for meaning and purpose by letting the world disciple them	Learn to recognize people who are searching for something better	Recognize Struggles: Home life Friends Personal Faith Ex Self-esteem 1. Identity 2. Belonging 3. Purpose
2. Listening to testimonies from others about what is working for them	John B Testifies that Jesus is the Messiah and points Him out in the crowd John 1:29-34	The world says alcohol, drugs, sex, power, control, money, possessions, entertainment, etc., will satisfy	Share my testimony of what I didn't find in the world and what I did find in a relationship with Jesus	Sharing Testimony: Teachers/Staff Pastors Peers Internet Social Media
3. Looking at the lives of those who are testifying about what they believe in	The disciples follow Jesus to see what he is like and Jesus says, "come and see" John 1:35-51	We see wealthy, famous people who have all these things of the world and are depressed and unhappy	Live a godly example that bears the fruit of someone truly connected to the Vine John 15:1-8 Gal 5:22-23	Modeling Faith: Integrity Fruits of the Spirit Consistency Truth Work ethic
4. Trying what others say is working for them	Disciples go with Jesus and live life together in dialogue and action together John 13:34-35	You try it anyway and find it satisfies only for a little while	Invite others to community and show them how to have a personal relationship with Jesus	Mentoring/discipling By faculty/staff/ pastors
5. Engaging in community with those who testify and they help you to become more like them	Disciples spend years in relationship with Jesus to learn of His beliefs and how to live them out (All 4 Gospels)	You try more because they tell you more is better and more will satisfy	Lead others into neighborhood outreach activities- -both humanitarian and spiritual (Book of Acts)	Outreaches/ Community Service Evangelism Counseling Nurturing Small groups Hobbies Accepting community
6. Sharing your testimony of what has worked for you and invite others to follow (You never know who may be searching...)	70 Disciples are sent out and then at Jesus' ascension all disciples (present/ future) are told to "Go" share a gospel testimony (1 John 1:1-4)	In your brokenness and emptiness you cry out for help and start the search again	Once others have encountered Jesus and His mission encourage them to become disciple-makers too	Organic sharing of testimony with: Peers Parents Testimony in church Social media Bring friends to groups and church

In my experience, a lot of what is written today about discipleship focuses primarily on step five outlined above, while missing some of the important elements listed there. In fact, much of discipleship has traditionally focused on Bible study, prayer, and maybe a few other spiritual disciplines, but I think it is very important to look at this whole process as part of *making disciples for Jesus*. This includes some elements that have traditionally been considered evangelism, but it also this involves a great emphasis on creating healthy relationships in our homes, schools, and churches, which will naturally flow outward to the community.

Activity for This Chapter

With a friend or small group, go through the six-step discipleship process. Share how you have seen each step lived out/fulfilled in your own life. As you share, try to bring out some details of your personality including specific characteristics and experiences that have had significant influence on who you are today and how you relate to God. Then, begin thinking through how this discipleship process has shaped your life, and who may have actually been discipling you through this, or how you may be actively discipling yourself.

Chapter 2

Who Discipled You: Stories from My Students

Just as I've asked you to consider who discipled you at the end of Chapter 1, I have also started asking this of all the students in my Collaborative Ministry classes. I've received more than one hundred stories this year and will continue to ask my students every semester because there are some amazing stories out there. I want to share some of them with you as encouragement. These stories come from diverse cultures and contexts around the world—beautiful stories and broken stories—but through it all, God has called and reached individuals so diverse, we can each find pieces of stories—if not whole stories—that we can relate to. The stories which follow are broken down in order according to the elements in the discipleship model discussed in Chapter 1.

Context of Searching: Dissatisfaction with Life and Seeking

CHIN-MAE

One of the people who discipled me was a pastor in Northern-Asia Pacific Division who also served as a coordinator of the missionary movement of which I was a part. I joined this missionary movement for one year because I wanted to get away from college for a while; in all honesty, it was a way for me to run away from my burnout. Through this pastor I learned how to have a personal relationship with Jesus by meditating on God's Word.

It was not merely a mentoring; he lived with us and shared his life with us so that we could see and learn what it looks like to live a life with Jesus. From that point on, I wanted to live like him and begin my own journey of becoming more like Jesus. It was through this newfound inspiration I realized it would not be so bad to become a minister. This was indeed a turning point for me.

FRANCISCO

The two people who took the time to disciple me were teachers from different Adventist schools. The first taught Bible at Auburn Adventist Academy in Washington, and the second was a chaplain/coach at Milo Adventist Academy in Oregon. The Bible teacher lived out the love of God and always entrusted me with things most people never would. I was causing trouble in my life during this time, yet this teacher showed up for me repeatedly. He taught me what it was like to stop and pray for any life situation, and he taught me what believing in someone looks like because he believed in me and spent time with me, allowing me to experience God's love in action.

The second teacher, a chaplain, constantly challenged and pushed me to do my best. It was like he could see something in me I could not see then. He would sit down and talk seriously with me about life after high school. He took me shopping and bought me clothes for a banquet so I would have attire which adhered to the dress code at the time. He was my basketball coach and placed me in a second classroom with him where I could learn about life lessons, hard work, dedication, and character-building.

God placed these two disciplers in my life when my relationship with my father was failing miserably. It wasn't until I was 21 that my father and I had a real relationship, and these two men were like second fathers during a time when I had no direction.

ESTEVAO

After high school, I started living the prodigal lifestyle, wasting my life away. I remember it being a life of parties and friends, but I was not happy—**nothing satisfied my emotional need** (Author's note: This is one of the key elements someone must possess to enter the discipleship process; emphasis mine). When I talked with my mother, she would always tell me she was praying for me. She was apprehensive she would never see me alive again.

I am sure that because of her many prayers, I started listening to the gentle yet powerful voice in my head asking me to get up and pray. I fought with that voice for many days. Then one night, I got up and prayed to God. I began reading the Bible. I began speaking with my mother more often, and then, I started reflecting on my life previously compared to the one I was living. I started to sing hymns from my childhood. "I'd Rather Have Jesus" was the hymn that made me think seriously about leaving the world and returning to Jesus, and I began to look for an Adventist church where I was living.

I found one, and though the church community was small, all of them became support beams God used to hold me up as I began my journey with him. I then began serving in different offices within the church, as youth director and praise team director. I gave many Bible studies as I worked with Bible workers and church members. God accepted me and began the healing process, using many of his disciples to make me a disciple.

Now I am a chaplain, helping others know about him–that they are not alone as they face life's travails. I teach about how good it is to trust in God as our Master and Redeemer.

Natural Curiosity: Listening to the Testimonies of Others for Answers

CHUNG-HEE

Growing up as an Adventist, I do not recall being discipled at a young age. It is a real shame because, looking back, I know it would have made a huge difference in my life. I mostly received discipleship from the world through entertainment and my peers. However, when I returned to God in 2011, God led me to be discipled under Elder Kim, a man of God in his 50s.

I did not really want to come back to the Adventist church because I did not remember people in the church being loving and faithful to the truth they had. However, I knew I needed to keep the Sabbath day holy if I wanted to be faithful to God, and going to a small home group rather than a full-blown church seemed more appealing.

When I first attended Elder Kim's small group, I was so shocked by the sermon because it answered the questions I had. I started observing people there very carefully; everyone there seemed sincere, devout, friendly, and welcoming. At that time, I was suffering from a lot of health problems, and everyone was very sympathetic to my situation. Elder Kim and his wife took me in as if I was one of their own family. They invited me to their home often even though they were struggling financially and had to work long hours. I knew there was something special about these people, and I opened up to them with my deepest troubles and sorrows.

Elder Kim and his wife used to run a home sanitarium back in Korea, helping people heal through natural remedies, all while leading them to Jesus, the Healer. Listening to all the healing stories gave me hope. Elder Kim and his wife treated me with different natural remedies for my severe occupational pain in my wrists, back pain from sitting long hours at work, and gut problems from my poor lifestyle. They listened to my stories and recommended changes which might help. As I changed my diet and my lifestyle according to their recommendations, my health issues started to go away.

Elder Kim's stories inspired me to dream of reaching people with my God-given talents. With newfound excitement, I met with all my friends and family members to share what I had been learning, but sadly, none of them were interested. However, at Elder Kim's small group, I learned how evangelism works, especially in the Korean immigrant community. I learned as I watched him connect with people, saw how he taught them, and how he dealt with their questions and challenges.

He often gave me opportunities to sit with him whenever new people came to his church, and gave me the chance to answer questions being asked. All this helped me to grow. Later, I was led to an English-speaking church, and there, my talents really flourished. I was involved in teaching and preaching, and later was asked to serve as an elder. I was able to use the training I received from Elder Kim at a whole new level.

To this day, I am very thankful to Elder Kim and his wife because they were willing to be used by God, sacrificing their time and energy to settle me into the truth, to train me, and to equip me for God's plans for me. They were like a father and mother to me. Even today, whenever I need wise counsel, Elder Kim is the first person I go to.

Looking for Consistency, Authenticity, and Meaning: Watching to See if Actions Match the Testimonies

MEI

There was only one person whom I truly believe discipled me throughout my college years. Arlene is a music teacher, choir director, and mission trip coordinator of Hong Kong Adventist College, serving there for over ten years. Because of her passion for ministry, she was the first person to initiate and start mission trips for her HKAC choir members. I was one of those choir members who had the privilege of serving on these mission trips.

Arlene not only lived her walk with Christ, but she was constantly patient, compassionate, understanding, and outspoken about things she was concerned about and cared for. Like Jesus, who trusted his disciples to preach the gospel on their own, Arlene trusted her students to serve Jesus through preaching and serving others without having any doubt in them. Whenever we had our pre-mission trip meetings, she constantly reminded us to mingle with the locals instead of sticking with our own team members. In fact, she herself followed this advice and deeply engaged with the local people, helping with their needs in any way she could. She encouraged us to hear people's stories and their struggles, pray with them, and invite them to our events. She didn't just talk the talk; in fact, I did see her walk the walk. She inspired me to be more inclusive, understanding, and loving in my ministry, encouraging me to be a disciple maker who is called to care.

DAL-RAE

Parents are meant to be nurturers who feed, raise, and teach their children proper behavior and attitudes. My mom took this role to a whole new level, discipling not just through parenting, but also through her lifestyle. Nine out of ten times I saw her, she was reading the Bible; she showed me how Christians should be connected with God daily outside of church. Therefore, I started reading the Bible, one chapter daily before going to school.

When I went to college, Mom texted me scriptures along with her personal testimony and spiritual advice every single day. I carried on the habit of reading the Bible every day, and even though I went to a non-Christian college, I successfully kept my faith and evangelized to my non-Christian friends who followed me to church instead of following the secular influences. Of course, there were some hard times in college; times when my spiritual life was shaky. However, my mom's prayers and demonstration of spiritual life kept my spirituality in place.

Mom valued spiritual success over academic success. She did not micromanage my life but demonstrated the true Christian life, always emphasizing seeking the kingdom of God first and offering your best to God.

I truly believe one's lifestyle and choices show the personal connection one has with God, and this will be key to leading children in keeping their faith when they leave home.

AMIRI

Thank God for David and Daniel. In the fall of 1993, I entered my sophomore year at university. Providentially, my two roommates were in their final year: two Adventist young men, David and Daniel. They were traditional Adventists but not extreme conservatives. David was a musician and singer; Daniel was a man of the Word. The power of their belief was evident in the way they lived their lives. They were very even-keeled and approachable, and though they did not travel extensively nor were they heavily cultured, they were well-read, giving them a big-world perspective. I cannot recall a moment when they became rowdy, un-Christ-like, quarrelsome, or overbearing. Instead, I found them courteous and willing to engage at my slow pace. I remember them engaging with God consistently, reflecting not just on the need to connect with God but also on enjoying spending time with God; they lived the principles they talked about. David and Daniel were heaven-sent, the conduits through which the Holy Spirit satisfied my cognitive yearnings. They discipled me back to Christ.

Though I grew up in a traditional conservative church, my father often had an alternative perspective to the rigid ultra-conservative beliefs held onto by his brother, the pastor. I have grown more and more appreciative of the softer side of Jesus in which my father believes, realizing now that his perspective is directly Bible-based.

My father does not make small talk a lot. However, when he speaks, his words are always with the salt of substance. Correspondingly, his attitude to discipline and instruction was continuously measured with grace. I can recall him using physical punishment on me only once; most of his reprimand was through conversation. My father's Christian nurturing approach, mainly without judgment, satisfied the emotional emptiness within me. He loves as he understands the love of Christ. My father discipled me.

Challenge to Try: Trying What Others Say and Do

FIDELINE

One of the persons who discipled me was my mother. My mother was and is still one of the most influential people on my faith. I grew up in an Adventist home, and even as a child I would observe my mother's relationship with God. She taught my siblings and I the importance of prayer and intimacy with the Lord. She instilled in me that all the Lord wants from us is to seek his face daily, to form a relationship with him, and I have always carried that with me.

The other person who has discipled me was my youth pastor Delvin Ferris, whom I met in my Haitian Adventist church. Although I grew up in the church, I did not fully understand the gospel's truth. Pastor Delvin took the time to explain the grace of God and what Jesus did on the cross, and the work of the Holy Spirit. He poured into me by giving me Bible studies and teaching me how to study the Word myself.

Pastor Delvin led the young people at my church, including me, on how to minister to people at the hospital, and I began to shadow him as he lived out his ministry at our church. He also helped me recognize my calling.

I had graduated from undergraduate studies and did not know what the Lord wanted me to do with my life. Pastor Delvin encouraged me to pursue chaplaincy; a calling I understood through watching Pastor Delvin work. As a pastor specializing in chaplaincy, he made himself available to the church, the young people, and me.

ATAMAI

I was discipled to Christ by my maternal grandmother who was a former Adventist. Through a series of family decisions, she and her husband left the church and became leaders of one of the main protestant denominations in Samoa. Nevertheless, much of my training at home was based on Adventist lifestyle principles, which I eventually recognized when I became a committed Adventist in my twenties.

Grandma lived out her devotions and relationship with God faithfully and joyfully—I just followed her example. I learned to love others because she loved others so well. She prayed unceasingly and led our daily family worships. Grandma was such an effective discipler because she imitated Christ to me, and in the process of imitating her, I became a follower of Christ!

Oddly, I learned to love God from a former Adventist, and without this love of God, I would not have become a committed Adventist. My mom became an Adventist in the United States, so when I came to care for her when I was 18, I was formally introduced to Adventism. I was baptized three times; the first time was to fulfill Mom's dying wish, the second time was a head decision after attending an evangelistic series (which unfortunately turned me into a bitter and lost legalist), and the final time because I cried out to God again like my grandma would in times of crisis. It was then that my childhood love of God became amazingly real.

There was no real discipling in my local church; I think they mistook evangelism for discipleship because the church focused on conducting annual evangelistic series. There was no follow-up after people were baptized. What the church did well was recognizing members' gifts and plugging them into the ministries where those gifts could be used.

However, there was no training, which forced me to read the church manual on my own. Yet, God in his infinite wisdom and providence appoints the places where we live so that in that community and in the events of our lives, we are brought closer and closer to him. Ultimately, discipleship is the work of God in us and through us.

MIHAILS

It was a community of people who discipled me. The first was Will, my Sabbath School leader when I was in the 8th grade. On one occasion, after giving my life to God at summer camp, I chose to try smoking weed with some friends. Afterward, I ran home to call Will, confessing what I had just done and feeling immense guilt. Will's response was, "First off, are you okay? Do you need me to call anyone?"

The way he handled the situation made me feel loved and not judged. Will was a strong, calming presence in my life, and having personally dealt with similar struggles to mine, he journeyed with me and was a pivotal part of my early spiritual journey.

The second person who discipled me is my friend Eric. He was a literature evangelist and Bible worker who led a Bible study at summer camp which changed my life. I attribute a lot of my success in ministry to him, as he always pushed me to reach excellence in all that I do. Eric was the first example of someone whose life I wanted to spiritually emulate.

As I matured in my walk with Christ, two men, Pastor Gary and Pastor Eddie, were a significant part of my discipleship process. Through their men's ministry program, I was able to rebuild my strained relationship with my father, go on the most epic mountain climbing experience of my life, and gain a vision of what I want my life and ministry to be like. When I questioned my call to pastoral ministry during my senior year of high school, Gary created a summer intern program at his church just for me that rekindled my passion for ministry.

Finally, someone who has journeyed with me since high school is my friend Oliver. He was my history teacher in 11th and 12th grade at Thunderbird Adventist Academy in Arizona. After my first year of pastoral ministry, I became the chaplain at Thunderbird and we got to work together. Oliver walked me through some of the most difficult times I had ever faced as a high schooler and professional during my time at Thunderbird. He's someone that I rely on for spiritual guidance still today, and my wife and I agree we would like to model our future family after his, due to his unfailing ability to prioritize God and his family above all else.

Commit to Community: Engaging in Community if it Seems to be Working

SEBASTIAN

My father was the first and most influential discipler in my life. He taught me the importance of prayer and reading the Bible daily. He also modeled a life of service and dedication to the church. I remember him always being involved in various church activities as a pastor and encouraging me to do the same.

The head elder of our church was another important discipler in my life. He was a wise and knowledgeable man who taught me about the doctrines and beliefs of Adventism. He would often invite me to his home for Bible studies and discussions about theology. Through these conversations, I developed a deeper understanding and appreciation for my faith.

The teachers and chaplain at my Adventist school also played a significant role in my spiritual development. They taught me about the importance of education and how it can be used to serve God, and provided opportunities for me to be involved in various service projects and mission trips. These experiences helped me see the importance of living out my faith in practical ways.

Lastly, my professor at the Adventist university where I attended taught me the importance of scholarship and how it can be used to further God's kingdom. He challenged me to think critically and to always seek truth, providing guidance and support as I navigated the challenges of college life.

GABRIEL

My journey in being discipled is split into four prominent figures. First, it all begins with my parents. They say your parents are your introduction to knowing who God is through their love. Of course, this makes the most sense in the ideal family in which I was blessed and fortunate to grow up.

In my early years, my father taught me about Jesus and how to pray. Every Friday night, we would sit by the couch, learn the Sabbath School memory verse of the week, and study the lesson. I had so many questions about life and the Bible, and my dad did an excellent job answering those questions.

My mother's faith allowed me to learn. There's nothing like a momma's prayers. After a long day of tasks, she would pray beside the bed on her knees for the protection and safety of our whole family. Today, when we speak on the phone, she never fails to say she is praying for me.

When I was 17, a new youth pastor was called to my home church. God put the pieces together because this youth pastor of mine cultivated many things which led to the assurance of my calling to ministry. This former youth pastor of mine took me under his wing and allowed me to preach my first full sermon. When I was ready to start studying theology at college, I felt very much equipped to embrace a new calling which would change my life forever.

Lastly, in the most mysterious ways, one prominent person who discipled me was my neighbor. We lived in the same apartment complex in L.A. He had kids the same age as me, and I saw him as a father figure. Eventually, his kids grew up and moved out of his home, but our friendship continued to grow. We would talk for hours about relationships, life, and sometimes God. Perhaps one would think that discipleship is only about the teachings of God and other spiritual topics, but during the most confusing times of my life, I believe the Spirit worked through my neighbor to navigate me through those difficult times.

After so many conversations, one day we openly talked about God (my neighbor wasn't a practicing Christian), and our conversation led him to pray and read the Bible. My neighbor's wisdom, love, and advice clarified my life at just the right times. I would conclude that even though he didn't have the same theological background as the other people in my life, he still saw me as a son and cared enough to help me grow.

Called to Care: Spontaneously Serving and Sharing What Has Happened

ANDREW

A year before I was born, my beloved mother was baptized into the Adventist Church, so I was fortunate to be born into an Adventist home. I would say that my mother was the first to disciple me. Despite all the negative circumstances we experienced in our family, such as my father's death, my mother was able to guide my steps on the path of salvation.

Someone else who discipled me was Heloisa, my Sabbath School teacher. She taught me to love Jesus and trust him, even when bad things happened. My teacher loved to tell Bible stories and motivate us to be faithful like the heroes of Scripture, but she taught us much more by her example than by the material she presented in Sabbath School. We could see she was in love with Jesus, as she exhaled the perfume of Christ's presence through her kindness, warmth, and patience in dealing with the noisy Sabbath School children.

Then, in my adolescence, my Pathfinders director helped disciple me. He taught us in practice about leadership, organization, and respect for authorities. It was in this Pathfinder club I heart the call to serve Christ as a pastor. I truly believe Pathfinder ministry is one of the best methods for discipling youth and teens.

In conclusion, looking back, I can say God sent many people to disciple me and still continues to send others help me in the process of improving in the service of the Lord.

HEITOR

I truly never had a mentor or pastor take me under their wing and show me the ropes of what being a pastor was all about. As a teenager and young adult, I was simply just another kid who attended church and vespers and then went home for the whole week without hearing from anyone at the church. However, there was a very special friendship I formed with an older classmate during my undergraduate years at Southern Adventist University in Tennessee that may just fall into this idea of discipling.

I have to say I did not like him at first because he seemed arrogant and harsh with his language. But one morning, I was involved in an accident which left me with bad front end damage to my car. I requested prayers for it, and this fellow student approached me after class. Turns out he had been a mechanic for years and knew a great deal about fixing cars. This single gesture turned into a friendship of discipleship.

He taught me everything I know now about auto mechanics, and he never charged me a single penny for the countless hours he spent working on my cars and teaching me. I vowed to pay it forward and I try to help people with my knowledge whenever the opportunity comes.

I may not have been discipled n a traditional sense, but I was discipled nonetheless. This former classmate of mine is now a pastor in the southwest, and we keep in touch on a weekly basis. If this is what discipleship is all about, then I can say with joy in my heart that I enjoyed it so much that I hope to be able to do the same for someone else one day.

One of the things I hope we can learn from the stories of my students in the pages here is that we don't know the stories each student carries with them as they come to school each day. Some are stories of love, others of neglect, and sometimes even varying levels of abuse. Still others have experienced great stories of spirituality and support. But the point is, we just never know what's going on behind the scenes, so we must be as sensitive, caring, and compassionate as we can be with all the young people we encounter as we try to care for and nurture each one with the time we spend and the stories we tell in their presence. In some cases, the stories from our journey with God may be the only stories of hope in Jesus they hear. You may be just the person the

Holy Spirit is leading into their lives for some sort of healing touch that day, and maybe you will be the person they talk about when they are one day asked, "Who discipled you?"

Activity for This Chapter

Think about individuals who have had an impact in your life, specifically individuals who discipled you. Then take a moment to answer the following questions:

What were some of the defining moments of their discipleship?

1. How did their discipleship impact how you yourself disciple others?
2. How did their walk with God impact your view of God and subsequent walk with Him?

I want to encourage you to write down your own discipleship story, drawing inspiration from the stories you have just read. After you've written your discipleship story, perhaps take it a step further and share it with the individual(s) who discipled you. Consider who you may be discipling right now and how they may describe your discipleship style in their own lives.

Chapter 3

Telling Our Stories to the Next Generation

The stories we tell are the testimonies we share. And the testimonies we share play a vital role in helping our children develop their identities. In the stories we tell about the adventures we live, are we including some tales about our adventures with Jesus? Do we talk about the great epiphanies we find in scripture and the answers to prayers we've experienced? Do we talk about the comfort and hope we find in our conversations with Jesus during hard times? Are we making sure kids know how they can experience these things too? This, I believe, is the great power of the teaching of the Shema for today's world.

> [4] "Listen, O Israel! The Lord is our God, the Lord alone. [a] [5] And you must love the Lord your God with all your heart, all your soul, and all your strength. [6] And you must commit yourselves wholeheartedly to these commands that I am giving you today. [7] Repeat them again and again to your children. Talk about them when you are at home and when you are on the road, when you are going to bed and when you are getting up. [8] Tie them to your hands and wear them on your forehead as reminders. [9] Write them on the doorposts of your house and on your gates."

I believe the Shema—at its best—is the sharing of stories like the ones we shared in chapter two. What could be more natural in conversation and more impactful to real life? Yes, we need formal classroom teaching, but the more organic sharing oftentimes drives the lessons home even more effectively.[1]

For the community of Christ, sharing these stories of faith within our mentoring relationships is one of the great things that turns them into discipling relationships, and it is also these stories which will help draw our children into the overall story of God that makes up our Adventist worldview. We must help our young people to not only know the stories of our faith, but they must also be led into a place of discovering their identity within the community of faith and how that identity can be nurtured and grown within the group. This will allow them to become valued citizens and leaders in the village of faith that is the church. Young people also need to see how their talents and gifts can benefit the group.

Forming this identity and belonging will help our children find their purpose in life as gifted members of the body of Christ. One of the best ways to drive these lessons home is to share our own experiences with and applications of scripture that have personally impacted us in meaningful ways. This is the testimony we have to share that will help protect our children from the lure of the testimonies and temptations of the world.

With this perspective I'd like to share another, more extensive, discipleship story to further illustrate the impact testimonies can have on relationships:

---

[1] Curt Thompson, MD. "Anatomy of the Soul, Surprising connections between neuroscience and spiritual practices that can transform your life and relationships," Tyndale Momentum, 2010, p. 81.

DELILAH

When I think of discipleship, there is one person who stands out above all the rest as a true example of discipleship. Her name is Lori. She is a pastor who may not be famous or well-known, but her ministry is deep and profound. The way she pours love into others is an example I want to emulate.

I have had to ask myself: What is it about her that makes her example of discipleship stand out? There are a few things I'd highlight. First, she has always been real, honest, and authentic. Second, she has treated me as family. Third, she helped me see the Gospel more clearly while speaking hope and truth into my life. And finally, she included me in ministry.

Because she's secure in her identity in Christ, Lori doesn't come across as someone who has all the answers or has it all together. Instead, she is honest and authentic. As our relationship grew, she told me I was like a daughter to her. She doesn't look down on me because I'm young enough to be her daughter; instead, she treats me as an equal co-laborer in ministry. She doesn't hide things or talk as if she had it all figured out, but talked about how she could do things better in her church.

Lori helped me understand the Gospel and gave me hope. When I went through a divorce, Pastor Lori walked through the valley with me. I felt I was responsible for the end of my marriage because I didn't take seriously the red flags I saw when we were dating. As she lived the Gospel in her conversations with me, Lori spoke glimmers of hope into me that God indeed still had a plan for me. I felt like a restless, broken, lost little girl trying to find my way.

When I was deciding whether or not to go to seminary, I looked back on a couple of ministry job opportunities I had turned down because they didn't seem like a right fit for me. I felt guilty for not working for God, as if I didn't deserve to go to school like everyone else. As I tried to see how God was leading me through the fog of many closed doors, Pastor Lori again spoke hope and positivity in my life. She helped me see the character of God in a more beautiful way, and how he was there for me and was working even in closed doors.

Lastly, she included me in both her life and her ministry. One example is when she invited me to attend a Bible study she was leading. I made quite a few comments during the study, and Pastor Lori told me later she could tell I would really enjoy giving Bible studies based on the comments I made.

What I have come to realize is that she saw me for who I was. I believe that speaking truth into the lives of young people is so important and has a profound impact. Pastor Lori spoke the truth of who I was, and of a gift God has given me leading/teaching Bible studies. She also included me in a ministry project she had helping a woman and her children move out of a house where they had been abused by the woman's ex-husband. It was a delicate situation, but Pastor Lori navigated with grace, wisdom, discretion, and kindness. Having the opportunity to do "get your hands dirty" in real life ministry with her was an invaluable experience.

One evening as I wrestled through my fears about going to seminary I realized I didn't have complete clarity, peace, or confidence about it. I already knew Pastor Lori believed I should come to seminary, and that she wanted me to have that life experience, as she had been through seminary herself, but she didn't push me. Instead, Pastor Lori listened and journeyed with me through the process. She was human with me. She talked through it with me. She said she would pray for me. The way she said she'd pray for me didn't make me feel as if she was looking down on me; her words were spoken in a tone of empathy, coming from a place of someone who understood how this was a struggle for me. I pray that one day I can disciple many young people in the way in which Pastor Lori discipled me.

Delilah's story is so inspiring because we see such committed care given to her by her mentor as she is discipled into the Gospel. I've spent 31 years in ministry to children, youth, and young adults who were born into Adventist homes but really didn't understand the gospel. In my experience, running student colporteur programs, children's ministries, youth ministries, young adult ministries, and yes, even teaching and ministering to seminarians, I have found most of the young people I have encountered within Adventism seem to understand the doctrines of our church better than they understand the Gospel. I once even served under a senior pastor who said, "The Gospel? The Gospel is for other Christians to teach—we have the 'truth'…We will teach the truth!" Discipleship must be Gospel-centered or it is not really discipleship at all.

The truth is that worldview begins forming from the earliest moments of a child's life and has important milestones that need to happen at each stage of life in order for them to build a strong Gospel foundation for correct doctrine to stand upon so that it doesn't devolve into abstract legalism. This is why we must begin sharing Gospel-centered stories of our faith with our children from birth. This is the best way to teach our children—educating them in the ways of the Lord—by following in the tradition of Jesus and other great teachers who followed the Shema by teaching with stories by the lakes and fields and pastures, using object lessons from the surrounding everyday scenes people knew and could relate to. This is known as a narrative approach to teaching scripture.

Examples in Scripture

In establishing a biblical narrative approach for educating young people from their earliest years, we can learn much from the apostle John, who said:

> We proclaim to you the one who existed from the beginning,[a] whom we have heard and seen. We saw him with our own eyes and touched him with our own hands. He is the Word of life. [2] This one who is life itself was revealed to us, and we have seen him. And now we testify and proclaim to you that he is the one who is eternal life. He was with the Father, and then he was revealed to us. [3] We proclaim to you what we ourselves have actually seen and heard so that you may have fellowship with us. And our fellowship is with the Father and with his Son, Jesus Christ. [4] We are writing these things so that you may fully share our joy.

This is the personal testimony of John which helps explain why he has written his Gospel stories the way he has, and perhaps even helps us understand why he would later use the vivid imagery he did when he described in great detail the movie-like narratives given to him in vision on the isle of Patmos and recorded in the book of Revelation. John's desire in his writings is to communicate the story of Jesus and how our lives can become a part of that story, too. That is why the calling of the disciples as we discussed in John 1 stood out to me as one of the best stories for helping us begin to understand the concept of true discipleship.

In John 1, we will remember that the invitation is to "come and see." It is to come and live. It is to come and follow in the footsteps of Jesus, learning his ways and following his example. It seems interesting to me that much of scripture, and almost all the teachings of Jesus, are in narrative form that actually "show" us how to live, and yet the majority of what has been taught in many Adventist classrooms and from many Adventist pulpits tends to be more doctrinal in nature. They tend more toward weaving a variety of scriptures together to form teachings rather than teaching through stories. Thankfully this is changing in many places, but we still have a long way to go and so setting forth this approach to scripture and method of teaching our children in the ways of the Lord is very important.

How We Lost Our Way

Have you ever thought about the stories of deep passionate love the founders of Adventism had for Jesus? Think about what kind of passion it must have taken to sell all your earthly possessions because you were so excited to be with Jesus. Try to imagine what it must take to give up all you have worked your entire life for. I love looking to find as many details as I can about their devotional lives and habits, which lit such passion. I think we have a general idea that they were passionate, but I really want to understand more fully how they fueled that passion and kept it alive. I would like to encourage you to spend some time looking for more inspiring stories in history and perhaps even in your own family—some stories that may have never even been told before—stories of faith and passion for Jesus.

With Adventist pioneer stories, we must keep in mind that fervor and passion were already in place during the great religious awakening which happened in America in the mid-1800s when the Millerite movement took place. And we must also keep in mind that it was this great passion for Jesus which led to the discovery of our denomination's doctrinal truths—not the other way around. I have a hard time believing all those sacrifices were made out of religious duty; it's much more likely they were made out of a passionate love for Jesus—just like the New Testament apostles who turned the world upside down because of their deep, loving experiences with Jesus and their subsequent on-fire relationships with him.

The core problem I see with our denominational approach to leading young people to Christ is that we have faithfully kept the great truths discovered during our denomination's founding but have somehow forgotten the passionate on-fire Gospel context which made the discovery of these truths possible. This is why we have a hard time sharing the gospel—even with our own children—because we are focused on holding up the pillars of truth rather than holding up Jesus, who is "the way, the truth and the life" (John 14:6)! Did you notice that the "way" comes before the "truth?" And the way I read it, way and life both have a strong reference to relationship theology and discipleship.

Let me be clear: I love the doctrines of our church which we fondly refer to as "the truth;" they are critically important because they paint the most beautiful and compelling picture of who God is and why we should love him. But if we fail to put the overwhelming emphasis on Jesus himself, the truth becomes irrelevant to the people we are trying to reach—including our own children. I see this as the great challenge before us in our church today: to put the gospel foundation back under the truth so that it can once again stand strong and stand tall.

How to Find Our Way

How do we put the gospel foundation back in place? The best opportunity is within the context of Christian education. The proper hermeneutic, for me, is a narrative Gospel-based hermeneutic, which is what we would call relationship theology, which is actually the story of God's love. That story lays a strong foundation for discipleship. Interestingly, it seems to me that Ellen White set this example herself by writing more on the life of Christ and the stories of his ministry than she wrote on any other topic. Additionally, her best-selling series, "Conflict of the Ages," tells story after story that reveal how God's story can mingle with human stories in the greatest story ever told—the story of redemption.

So, as we continue to look at stories, we must remember that discipleship happens according to the Shema found in Deuteronomy 6. Every day, all day long, children are learning about their world. If we are teaching them the ways of God and sharing the stories of his love, that is what will win their minds and prevail. But, on the other hand, if we fail to daily teach children born into Adventist homes the stories of God, then the stories the world is telling in innumerable ways and means will take precedence. In society today, where many families have both parents working, it is more important than ever to put our children in places where they can be discipled all day long by loving Christians who teach from a Gospel worldview as a foundation for life and truth—this is the only way we can hope to keep our kids with us in this world and in the world to come.

It is important to clearly understand that every environment children are in attempts to disciple them into its way—there are no neutral environments in the world. Businesses want to disciple us into materialism; influences want to disciple us into godlessness; the list goes on. Especially in a capitalist society, everyone seems to be wanting to sell us whatever it is that they are producing to increase their bottom line by telling us stories of how happy we will be if we buy into their philosophy. We must be very careful and discerning about the influences we allow into the lives of our children. This is where a Gospel focus can help us be discerning in the decisions we make regarding the lives of our children, and this is where a narrative hermeneutic can help guide us along the way. If our young people cannot see how the story of scripture fits into the story they are living on a daily basis, they have great difficulty seeing the importance and relevance of being Christian. Being Adventist will, in turn, seem even more distant from the practical realities of life.

With this in mind, narrative is the primary hermeneutic I'm focusing on in relation to working with young people. Jens Brockmeier and Hanna Meretoja agree with this approach when they say, "…we propose viewing narrative as a hermeneutic practice in itself, a practice of meaning-making. This practice—or perhaps better, this plethora of practices—is of crucial significance for complex processes of interpretation which underlie, for instance, our ideas of self and identity." This is especially important to remember considering that finding self and identity are one of the primary tasks young people face. Our goal is to help our youth find this identity in the Gospel story of Jesus Christ within the Adventist community of believers.

Activity for This Chapter

Write down your own personal story/testimony in a journal. As you start writing your own testimony, you will start to see how God has gifted you with your own personal story/testimony to share with the younger generation. Pray that the Lord will open your eyes, ears, and heart to share this story when the Holy Spirit prompts you.

Chapter 4

Finding Your Story Through Three

It is very interesting to me that one of the best passages—my favorite that helps me keep discipleship in mind throughout the day—is found in the Old Testament. But when you think about it, discipling didn't begin in the New Testament. It began with Jesus coming to the Garden of Eden to walk and talk with Adam and Eve, creating animals while Adam named them according to their characteristics. God was teaching Adam and Eve to tend the garden and all his ways of creating and enhancing the beauty that surrounded them. He was also warning them of the dangers in their world. Curt Thompson, in his book "Anatomy of the Soul," also brings out this beauty in scripture when he says:

> That is why I believe that faithfully telling and listening to our stories is one of the single most important things we can do as followers of Jesus. Storytelling inevitably engages our memories—both the speaker's and the hearers'—and so opens the door to a different future. The Bible is so powerful in part because it contains the story of creation, rebellion, redemption, and recreation, all of which are told in the rich, messy, beautiful, tragic, hopeful tapestry of the lives of God's ancient people.[1]

---

[1] Curt Thompson, MD. "Anatomy of the Soul, Surprising connections between neuroscience and spiritual practices that can transform your life and relationships," Tyndale Momentum, 2010, p. 81.

As an example, this is how my narrative educational hermeneutic works in my approach to Psalm 23 in my seminary classroom. I use a three-story approach: First, we must understand David's story (the context), then I share my story (how I apply the text to my life), then I send my students out to reflect and find their story (how they apply the text to their lives). This passage and the example of my application of it can draw them closer to God and have an impact on the way they interact with the world around them. Simply put, it's His: His (God's/Biblical) story, my story, and their story. This is perhaps the most important part of my Gospel narrative approach to scripture; we must see our story *within* God's story, and we must understand our story *through the lens* of God's story, and then share our God-impacted story as it intersects with the stories of those we meet.

The Gospel story must be at the center, discipleship is the process, and a life-changing personal relationship with Jesus is the end goal. I believe keeping these three ideas in mind as we study scripture and soak in it devotionally, they will help keep us on track. A true understanding of the purpose and meaning of scripture will help us lead our children to Jesus to find their own identity in him.

An Example Using Psalm 23

In my seminary classes, I take my students through Psalm 23 phrase by phrase, first looking at what it meant to David (his story), then sharing what it means to me (my story). Then I give the students reflective time to consider all they have just discovered and make a personal application by journaling what it means to them (their story). Below I will walk you through this process. Due to the limits of space, we will look only at the first phrase of Psalm 23. And actually, we really only cover the first two words: the Lord.

"The Lord is My Shepherd"

HIS STORY

The first thing in considering the context of this passage is who David was and who "the Lord" was to him in his experience. Scripture is full of stories that give us great detail into the life of David. From his boyhood days with the sheep in the fields, to his tragic mistake with Bathsheba, we see a man of passion—passionate for God and for everything he put his hand to. Even though he was mighty in battle, David was also passionately in love with his Lord as expressed in many psalms.

My favorite Psalms of David's passion are Psalm 63, where David talks about lying awake all night thinking about his Lord and desiring to be with him, Psalm 27, where he states that he wishes he could just go and live in God's house forever, and, my personal favorite, verse 8 of Psalm 27 (NLT), where David says, "my heart has heard you say, 'come and talk with me.' And my heart responds, 'Lord, I am coming,'"

Psalm 18 shows us an incredible display of who the Lord is to David as he pictures him coming down from heaven to save him in battle. In this passage, David sees God the way he needs his God—as a mighty warrior riding the back of a mighty angelic being breathing fire and smoke as he, "shot his arrows and scattered his enemies (Ps 18:14)." So when David says, "the Lord," this is who the Lord was to him—a mighty Savior/Warrior who was constantly at his side.

They shared such an intimate bond that David is referred to in scripture as a "man after God's own heart" (1 Samuel 13:14). It is a rather interesting picture that scripture paints of David as a shepherd/poet/musician/warrior/lover, and we need to understand this if we want to attempt to understand the passionate complexity of the relationship of dependence David had on the Lord as he attempted to make the Lord his Shepherd on a daily basis. And this is a key point: David had to *choose* his Shepherd every day. One day's choice does not prevent the next day's failure; we all live one day at a time.

MY STORY

After reflecting on these things, it is imperative for me to sit and think about who God is to me. Before I can really grasp my relationship with him, I must imagine who I think he is because my understanding of the very nature of God to a large extent determines what that relationship will look like. And so, I think back to the days of my youth when I lost my way and fell into the college party scene, somewhat like the prodigal son, and how God showed up in the middle of my drunkenness with a vision in the night and gave me a very personal visit and calling that drives me in my mission and ministry to this day. I also have to think about how God created me as a right-brained artist who longs for a relationship with God but has less natural inclination and drive to understand the more cognitive prophecies of Daniel and Revelation. The beauty is that Jesus knows me, he knows how he created me, and he knows how he can best show himself to me. He knows the picture of himself I will respond to the most positively, and he knows exactly how to Shepherd me in exactly the way I need, just as he shepherded David in just the way *he* needed.

THEIR STORY

As a pastor and teacher, it is my responsibility to challenge my students to understand who they are, who God created them to be, and how they may find him most fully in their relationships with him. We are all created differently, and we all have different needs in our relationships with God. This means that, as a teacher, I have to be willing to allow a great deal of diversity of thought as there are so many personalities and experiences that are so different from mine.

My goal is always to share my story and journey, and to hold up the countless stories of scripture so my students can find the ones which inspire them to follow after God as well. I try my best to be a guide and to accept those stories to which I cannot relate or fully understand. There is certainly a need to uphold a strong doctrine of who God is and the distinctive truths which reveal his character, but from there is a world of nuance we must each spend a lifetime pursuing individually. We must also pursue this nuance corporately as we share the journey together with our stories (His, Mine and Theirs) intertwined in community as the body of Christ.

Every semester I help my students experience the power of Three-Story by creating their own Three-Story worship talk in class. They partner up and I change the approach just a bit to make it fit a classroom or chapel setting. Instead of starting with His Story, I have them start with My Story. I also did this with dozens of academy and junior high students so they could learn how to put together a worship talk for their peers, and sometimes even for sharing at church. I always have them share a story of something funny that happened to them personally.

Once they have that story, they have to find the moral of the story they want to bring out. Once the moral of their

My Story has been identified, I have them find a His Story which teaches the same moral. Then they practice good story-telling techniques. The Their Story portion is the final application for the listener.

To help this all make sense, here is an example from one of my students in academy back when I was a youth pastor. The student had an amazing My Story, and I suggested Psalm 18 as the His Story. I am including it here so you can see the application of Psalm 18 we discussed briefly earlier in this chapter.

MY STORY

When I was a little kid like seven or eight years old, I used to go to my grandma's house for sleepovers, and if you go to Grandma's house, you know it's the most fun you can imagine, right? I was at Grandma's house for a sleepover, and I decided to get up really early on Sunday morning to watch cartoons. Do any of you like cartoons? Oh I love cartoons! When I was a little kid, my favorite show was Scooby-doo. Any Scooby-doo fans out there?

So, picture this with me: I'm at Grandma's house sitting in front of the TV—you have to understand that Grandma had a really old TV, like three feet wide, two feet tall, and two feet deep; it's one of those old tube-type televisions. She had it on this little old TV stand (maybe it was good at one point in time but when I was there watching TV, it was really rickety and not very stable). So I'm up before Grandma, watching Scooby-doo, and I want to try and have it be like all big screen and surround sound so I'm sitting right in front of the TV, like one foot away from it. The episode was of Scooby-doo on an adventure in a cave somewhere, when all of a sudden, a monster jumped out.

When I saw the monster, it startled me so much that I hurled back and my legs hit the TV stand. The TV stand started wobbling and moving, and then suddenly, it fell forward right on top of me!

There I was, my skinny, scrawny little six-year-old body, being attacked by a massive old TV. I could hardly move, and my arms and legs were flailing. I started screaming: "Grandma! Grandma! Help!" Out of the corner of my eye, I saw Grandma running down the hallway, her long white robe billowing in the wind as she ran. In an instant, she swooped in, grabbed that TV with superhuman strength, and lifted it off of me and saved my life! It's just amazing what grandmas can do when they're in a desperate situation to save their grandchild!

HIS STORY

So, just like Grandma saved me in my distress, it reminds me of a story in the Bible when King David was saved from his distress. He was on the run from his enemies and, David being a mighty man of God—a warrior—he pictured God as a warrior too, because that's what he could relate to. In Psalm 18, David is crying out to God and this is what he said, starting in verse four: "The ropes of death entangled me, floods of destruction swept over me, the grave wrapped its ropes around me, death laid a trap in my path." But he continues, "In my distress I cried out to the Lord; yes, I prayed to my God for help, he heard me from his sanctuary, my cry to him reached his ears."

Now get ready for this. This is the scene where he pictures God up in heaven hearing his cry, and this is what David says in verse seven:

Then the earth quaked and trembled, the foundations of the mountain shook; they quaked, because of his anger, smoke poured from his nostrils, fierce flames leaped from his mouth glowing coals…He opened the heavens and came down on dark storm clouds; he rode mounted on a mighty angelic being, he flew soaring on the wings of the wind; he shrouded himself in darkness, veiling his approach with dark rain clouds. Thick clouds shielded the brightness around him and rained down burning hail and coals; the Lord thundered from heaven, the voice of the Most High resounded amid the hail and burning coals, he shot his arrows, scattered his enemies, great bolts of lightning flashed, and they were confused."

Is that amazing or what?

THEIR STORY

Just as David pictures God coming down to save him in the middle of his distress, and just as my grandma swooped in and saved me from a TV, God can be there for you, too. Now I'm going to guess you're not going to be attacked by a TV anytime soon like I was, but whatever it is you're facing in life, whatever it is you're afraid of or that's bothering you, you can cry out to Jesus and he will be there for you. I'm not going to say it's going to be an instantaneous miracle like with my grandma or what David pictured as a warrior, but he will be there for you to bring comfort and to bring help in some way. We don't know what that's going to look like but we can trust that he is faithful and he will walk beside us through the valley of the shadow of death, as David talks about in Psalm 23. He is always with us and many times he's even carrying us without us realizing it.

Activity for This Chapter

Now it is your opportunity to use the Three-Story method. This process is most enjoyable with a friend or someone who can listen as you share your story, and can help you sculpt the three stories together.

First, share a funny story that has happened to you. Craft the story to provide as many visual and audio effects for the listener. Then, find a Bible story which relates to the story you just shared, or addresses a similar principle or point. Open up the Bible story the same way: engagingly and creatively. Lastly, make it applicable to our lives today and especially to the lives of your listeners, if you are sharing publicly. Answer the question: How do these two stories, and/or the main principle hidden within, impact/affect our world and lives today?

Practice through this process until it becomes natural and easy, and then share it with someone new. This is an excellent way to practice storytelling.

Chapter 5

Why Campus-Based Ministry is Important in Forming Worldview

I believe one of the most important things we must keep in mind as we are trying to reach our own youth is that we must become cross-cultural missionaries. It's true, isn't it? All of our children are growing up in a much different world than we did, and even as a youth pastor who was close to a lot of kids, the reality is that though they wanted me to be involved in much of their world, there were areas where they wanted to go with their friends only—places I would not understand or navigate well. I heard stories of some of the deep, dark corners of the internet with unspeakable content that kids felt peer-pressured to explore. Places where adults were not allowed. When I ran Christian clubs on public school campuses, I'd hear about the weekend parties with drinking and drugs. One month, every weekend, all the rage was Ouija boards! Kids who had never come to my Christian club before were showing up with eyes wide as saucers asking what that other-worldly presence was that they had seen and felt. Really scary stuff!

We cannot be with our kids at all times and everywhere they go; this is why it is so important that our discipleship process establishes a strong Christian worldview we can help them apply in the real world. It is critically important that we help them apply faith in the areas of their lives where we are allowed and can have impact so they will have a better idea of how to apply their faith to the places where we cannot go with them.

This is why I believe in discipling kids on campus. For school-aged children, this is where they spend the majority of their waking hours and where they feel a lot of the peer pressure they face in life. This is where they are trying to fit in and find community. This is where they are forming their identity. This is where they are meeting the companions with whom they will travel life's roads—at least for a few years. And this is where they will hear many competing testimonies about what will make them happy and where they will be offered places of belonging in a world the internet has made more and more lonely.

As a long-term youth pastor, I can attest to the fact that this is one of the most difficult times of a young person's life—especially in junior high and high school. What I have found is that by showing up at school, I have the privilege of entering into a part of students' lives I never see at church. When I sit down for a lunchtime visit on campus with kids from my church and I ask them about their world, I hear stories I've never heard before. I get to see where kids are spending their time and who their friends are during the week. (Sometimes the weekday friends are much different than the weekend church friends.)

Being at school is a great place to practice the principles of the Shema. As they share stories of the struggles they face, I can share testimony by relating stories of encouragement from scripture and from my own application of biblical principles to the troubles I have faced in my own life. This is a great opportunity for the Three-Story approach to witnessing to our kids. In this application, it's *listen* to their story, then *share* my story and his story. It also gives me an opportunity to show I care—just by showing up—which demonstrates that I am trying to live a life consistent with what I say my testimony is. This helps kids try what I've been teaching them by applying biblical principles to real life as outlined in the first four steps of the discipleship process outlined in Chapter 1:

1. Recognize student's struggles
2. Share testimony
3. Model faith/fruits of the Spirit
4. Build discipling relationships
5. Create community with students
6. Students naturally share what impacts them

Additionally, visiting kids at school helps us to implement step five of the discipleship process. Campus is a great place to gather with a few kids at a time to form a Christian community with others who are trying to follow Jesus as well. This helps to form a Christian subculture within the greater secular culture for our kids in public schools, and perhaps a discipleship group that wants to go deeper into devotional life and living faith on campus at a Christian school. I've personally done both. Research shows there are dramatically fewer at-risk behaviors in kids attending Adventist schools[1], but even our own church schools do have some challenging influences to navigate. We must realize there is no perfect culture this side of heaven—wherever there are people, there is temptation of one kind or another. So, inviting students into campus clubs and groups helps them find positive friends and a safer place to find community. It also adds to the influence of

---

[1] For more on this see the Institute for Prevention of Addictions at Andrews University website: https://www.andrews.edu/services/ipa/index.html

the community we form in our youth groups at church as outlined in step five of the discipleship process.

Kids, like adults, learn very early how to compartmentalize. They put church things in one compartment, school things in another compartment, and internet life in yet another. All these compartments and competing voices can become quite confusing and lead to a lot of distress if we don't find a way to help weave a Christian worldview and narrative through them all. Like I said before, we can't be with our kids everywhere they go but I've found that by showing up to visit with them at school, I get the chance to become more relevant to more of their world, and help them take one more step in applying faith to life. This can help young people make further application when they are alone with their friends.

Often during lunch-time visits, when taking prayer requests, kids want to talk about their weekend experiences and mistakes—after the fact. It is critically important to be there and be able to discuss these experiences so they will hopefully do better the next time they face peer pressure to do something that goes against the values of the worldview they are encountering at church and at home.

Here is a story from one of my students which helps to illustrate the importance of students having friends in their journey of discipleship. Once again, they need to develop the ability to navigate the world when the adults who have been discipling them aren't there. In this story, the close friend also happens to be a brother, helping his sister navigate a world their parents just could not understand:

BLESSING

I am a pastor's kid (PK) so I was raised in a Seventh-day Adventist home. My parents were great people who loved me and did everything they could for my brother and me to be spirituality rooted in the Christian faith, with a well-rounded, loving, and safe upbringing. They encouraged both my brother and me to have ownership of our faith and personal journeys with God. We had worship as a family every day and both my brother and I were encouraged to lead worship and engage in Bible studies, providing us with a strong biblical foundation.

As I grew older, however, it was evident that the generational gap between my parents and I was increasing. I grew up in a culture which questioned everything while they did not. I grew up in a culture which rebelled against tradition, while they embraced tradition and saw it as part of their Christian identity and experience. This is where my brother stepped in and discipled me in a beautiful way.

I appreciated his discipleship style, which was to validate my feelings, questions, and frustrations about our church and faith. He never tried to make excuses or make me feel like I was the problem for the resentful feelings I had toward certain injustices at church; he would even sometimes share his own concerns about his faith and the church. He was always fully present.

One time I was going through a hard time and he showed up at my university with two gifts: one was a beautiful dress, and the other was a notebook. In the notebook it said, "Bless, I know you are going through a difficult time. Remember that God sees your pain. Use this diary to write to him about your frustration, pain, and feelings; he wants to hear from you." These were probably the most meaningful gifts I have ever received.

My discipleship story isn't about leaving the church or having a dramatic turnaround in my life; it is about someone being present when I had doubts; someone who validated my emotions and my humanness, and empathized with me. While discipleship is about mentoring and advising another, it is also about sharing our humanness and limitations with each other. It can even be about having conversations about uncertainty, sadness, discouragement, and doubts as Christians. It is having a safe space to be transparent without feeling judged. That was and is what my brother is for me. Today I am in ministry hugely because of him and the encouragement of my parents.

You are What You Love

One of the best resources I have found for helping leaders understand how to help form a young person's worldview is written by James K.A. Smith called, "You are What You Love."[2] The most impactful part of Smith's message can be found on YouTube under the same title as the book. The basic message Smith shares, and the one that seems most impactful to the groups of seminary students and denominational leaders I've shown it to, is his point that a person is not a brain on a stick.

---

[2] James K.A. Smith (2016), "You are What You Love: the Spiritual power of habit," Brazos Press, Grand Rapids, MI (a division of Baker publishing group).

In this illustration, Smith holds up his forearm vertically with his fist clenched and points to his fist as if it is the brain. He says that Christians often think that they can change a person by pouring correct information into the brain (as he points to his fist). Then he goes on to talk about how so many of us have experienced spiritual highs at retreats where we have learned something new about God or the Bible that has transformed our thinking and understanding. He talks about how we all go home vowing to be changed persons, but after about 3-4 days, the spiritual high has worn off and we are back to being our old selves. His point is that information alone does not change us—there is a huge gap between the head and the hand. Most people do not act on what they know as much as they act on what they love.

This is why Smith says discipleship must focus on helping people fall in love with Jesus, because it is actually the heart that controls the hand, which represents behavior/actions. Smith goes on to say that habits are the key to helping us in nurturing our relationship with Jesus, which in turn is powerful in determining what we love and how we act. Smith states that we are primarily lovers rather than thinkers, and we go about our lives in the world following what we love. With this assumption, the main question Smith likes to ask people is, "What do you want?" This is the same question Jesus asked the disciples who began following Him in John 1:38.

The world has mastered making people desire what it has to offer, which is why many people spend their time pursuing some version of the "good life" they have seen on TV or online. The world has mastered the art of storytelling and luring people (including and especially young people) into the beautiful narratives it creates. This is why one of the most important things we can do in discipling our children is help them fall in love with Jesus and the meaningful lives they can live with him.

This is the power of using story to present our worldview, especially knowing that competing worldviews are actively pursuing our children 24/7 via a myriad of influences. Being with our kids on campus where they live their lives on a daily basis gives us influence in the spaces where temptations come more frequently and where faith must make sense in action. If kids can't apply faith to life and experience in the real world, it will never become their own and it will have no ability to guide the choices they make.

Smith talks about the power of habit being very important. Habits are the foundation of devotional life and discipleship, and it is critically important that we help our young people form good habits in many areas of life, but especially in regards to their spirituality. We will talk more about devotional habits in the next chapter, but for now, as we wrap up this chapter on shaping our young people's worldviews by being present on campus, I want to highlight the importance of simply being spiritually present. The first story happened at an Adventist academy; the second is from an Adventist university.

JOSUÉ

I grew up in a very religious home. Our family was always doing devotionals, family worships, and studying the Sabbath School lesson together. I grew up learning about the Bible and Jesus, and I began to know about God and Bible stories at a young age, but it was all just knowledge for me. My parents did a great job of helping me develop Bible knowledge, but it wasn't until I went to academy that I developed a real relationship with Jesus.

In academy, my youth pastor and chaplain, Russ, was someone who, from the beginning, discipled me. He intentionally got to know my sister and I, and it was so great getting to know and feel comfortable around him. He was always approachable and intentional in his ministry to the youth at church and school. I could always ask him the questions I had, and he was open to hearing anything I had on my mind.

Seeing how he cared about everyone both on and off the pulpit, in his office, on school trips, on mission trips, and in Bible studies showed me how loving and caring he was. He showed the love of Jesus in everything. He always treated young people with kindness; I always saw his intentionality in building loving relationships on mission trips and outreach events.

Once I became an upperclassman, he led me through a series of Bible studies so that I could also give Bible studies to others. He saw my desire to share my faith and fed into that. He helped me to develop Bible studies so I would be ready to give Bible studies to other young people who asked for them. I ended up giving Bible studies that he and I had worked on together to several young people who then got baptized.

Russ has been there for me through the highs and lows in life and has been okay with my doubts and frustrations. He helped me develop my ministry before I ever decided to do full-time ministry, and he helped me develop my passion for service, and he continues to disciple me to this day.

VICTORIA

The poster child for Adventist education, I attended Adventist institutions from daycare to undergraduate and now graduate school. However, my relationship with God was all memorized Bible verses, spoon-fed biblical practices, and social restrictions. It wasn't personal; only ritual.

To preface, I have to paint the picture of the kind of undergraduate I was. In short, I began my bachelor's degree pursuits at Andrews University at the tender age of 17, where I was highly impressionable and lacking in self-confidence, severely depressed, and juvenile in my spiritual walk. In an effort to find both community and myself, I self-medicated with extracurricular activities and events outside of the classroom. While I was failing classes, I was excelling in community service, student government, volunteering, activism, and anything I could do seemingly mindlessly. I didn't want to confront my indecisiveness with academia, my fear of failure (which at that point was an academic reality), financial and mental health difficulties, etc. In short, I was a train wreck before the crash.

It was vespers on a Friday night, in the thick of winter term. Many students crammed into this sacred space, this common ground for believers, worship, and co-curricular credit to meet the omnipotent God. As the band and singers led students into adulation to God, I found myself weeping in my seat. I was inconsolable and as my friends swelled around me, I didn't have the language to express with words what the Spirit was convicting me of. Within the crowd of weeping students and worship, she saw me. Seemingly out of nowhere, she peered out from behind me and asked me, "Are you okay?" That was the beginning of my discipleship journey.

She attended the seminary, was praise team leader for New Life Fellowship, and had the anointing of God on her life and ministry. At the time, I was not aware that I needed someone in my life to show me how to serve God, how to love him during difficult times, and how to be transparent in my walk with him. I saw how she lived for God and how she was blessed beyond the material things, and I knew I needed something. That something would be God, and she introduced me to him, intimately.

When my discipler found me that night in vespers, I was searching for love, affirmation, hope, community, and did I mention love? At the time, I was in a dark, difficult place and she was there for every tear, phone call, and meeting. She listened to where I was and showed me where I could be. She included me in her friend groups, which meant I now had a community of believers.

She was the discipler I didn't know I needed. She saved my life when she graciously walked into it. Thanks to her obedience to God and God's timeless grace and love for me, I have a story to tell.

These stories illustrate that living out the Shema with our kids on campus doesn't mean we have to give a Bible study every time we see them or talk with them—it simply means that we share testimonies and stories of our faith organically when we are spending time with them. It's really the overflow of "praying without ceasing." As they share difficulties and challenges in life, we can share our own success and failures in our attempts to live our lives with God. It can be a time of inspiration and praying together— not just for answers or simple solutions, but simply to share the journey and to offer love, support, and community.

On any campus where I have ministered, I have always ended up with groups of students who are trying, and failing, and trying again in life with Jesus. And wherever we have gathered together, more students have shown up and been very happy to find a group with similar values and goals to their own. This has been true on church school campuses and even more so on public campuses where so many influences are not Christian and some are absolutely antagonistic to Christianity.

Jesus called the many different parts of the body of Christ to come together to become whole and viable as a place to belong where identity and purpose can also be found. In my experience, being on campus where kids are actively living life is the best and most needed place for this type of discipleship according to the teaching of the Shema.

Activity for This Chapter

As you have read this chapter, I hope you have seen how important a spiritual presence is for discipleship. This chapter's activity is focused on getting involved.

How could you get involved in your local school? Could you start a small group with the youth in your community? Could you start a small group aimed at a specific emphasis (age, activity, worship focus, Bible book study, etc.)? Could you start a group of church members who intentionally reach out to the students and youth to let them know they are loved?

Start writing down some ways you could get involved and make your spiritual presence known to the young people around you.

Part 2

Devotional Life as the Center of Discipleship

This topic—to me—is the heart and soul of spiritual leadership and discipleship. In my experience, many people do not know how to approach devotional life. But what I've always told people working in ministry is that if your relationship with Jesus is vibrant and strong, you always have something to share; just talk about your latest devotional time or conversation with Jesus. Sharing openly and spontaneously from the heart is what I believe to be the core of the Shema. We shouldn't have to prepare material for every interaction with young people. Ideally, we should be so confident in our relationship with Jesus that we can just rely on the Holy Spirit to help spiritual conversation flow out of us and into the lives of kids.

Having God's Heart

The highest compliment in scripture is when David is called a man after God's own heart—not after God's own mind. Jesus said all the law and the prophets can be summed up by, "Love the Lord your God with all your heart, mind, and soul, and your neighbor as yourself." The "Love the Lord" part is also at the heart of the Shema. Jesus' final questions to Peter quoted at the end of the gospel of John are, "Do you love me? Do you love me? Do you love me?" In John 13:35,

Jesus said that our love for one another would prove to the world that we are his.

James K.A. Smith discusses how in Ephesians 3 Paul says, "I wish your 'love' would abound—so that you can know," which makes sense because Paul didn't really "know" the meaning of scripture until he was converted to a loving relationship with Jesus on the road to Damascus. It wasn't until Paul was converted that he fully understood the law and the prophets and immediately committed his life to sharing that love with the entire Gentile world. Paul's stated desire is that we could understand how wide and deep and long and tall God's love really is—it's like he is trying to tell us how huge and three-dimensional God's love is so that we can fully immerse ourselves in it!

If Jesus were to ask you, "Do you love me?" What would you say? How do we love Jesus? The primary goal of devotional time is to develop and grow our love and devotion to Jesus—but it's certainly not a one-size-fits-all activity. Studying doctrinal truths of scripture is definitely more objective because the Bible's teachings are quite consistent. Devotions, however, are supposed to nurture one's personal relationship with Jesus, rather than our rational understanding of who he is. We all have varying relationship needs based on our personality types, learning styles, and love languages. In other words: devotional time is a bit more subjective and personal, or at least it should be if we want to have the closest relationship with Jesus we are each capable of. The way I see it is that doctrine provides the framework for our relationship with Jesus. It tells us who he is and what kind of relationship he wants with us. But devotional life is the relationship which lives within the framework. We need both framework and relationship, but the ultimate goal is the loving connection with Jesus that sees us through the trials and joys of this life and is the thing that should make us contagious to those around us. The relationship should be the highly visible thing others see, are drawn to, and want for themselves.

Obviously everyone's marriage relationship and other friendships look somewhat different from person to person, and our relationship with Jesus will vary accordingly. In fact, the things we do to nurture and grow our human relationships can give each of us some vital clues as to how we can each deepen our personal relationship with Jesus. This is why devotional activities can sometimes be so controversial and misunderstood. Of course, there are some common elements we should all be engaging in during our devotional times, but the way we do so can vary greatly.

The goal of this chapter is to consider some of the variables to look at in structuring one's devotional time, because if we can't find our own devotional language and style, we will certainly struggle to help the young people we are discipling to find theirs—and chances are that if our young people can't have meaningful communication with Jesus, they may think it's not possible, and give up and walk away.

Chapter 6

My Story and Devotional Life

I revealed a bit about myself in chapter 1 and I'd like to begin this chapter by sharing a bit more, because if you know a bit more about me, it will help you understand why my devotional life looks the way it does. In chapter 8, my wife, Sarah, will be sharing a bit of her story and—in light of her personality and experiences—how she personally connects with God. My hope in sharing is that you will feel comfortable embracing who you are in Christ and how you may be able to deepen your own experience with God as you open yourself up to him more intimately.

You already know a bit about my experiences growing up and how they helped shape me, but here I want to focus more on my hobbies and interests because they can tell a lot about what I love and how I approach life, which directly informs how I approach my relationship with Jesus. We all need to try our best to know and understand ourselves and then accept and love ourselves for who we are because Jesus commanded us to "love our neighbors as ourselves." If we don't love and accept ourselves, we cannot do well at loving others! This will also help us lead the young people whom we are discipling to learn to love and accept themselves—which can often be quite a task during the turbulent years of adolescence.

When I left California after serving as a youth and young adult pastor there for 20 years and accepted the call to teach at the Seminary, it meant I was moving a lot closer to my childhood home in Minnesota. During all the years I lived in California, I rarely made it back to Minnesota because it was difficult to travel all that distance while raising three kids and managing all the expenses that go with that. So, moving to Michigan meant I was only a 10-hour drive away from Dad and the glorious junkyard I roamed as a boy. During my first year living in Michigan, I decided to go visit my dad for his 81st birthday in August, just before school started.

I was divorced at the time, and my daughter, Erin, was living with me, so it was just the two of us on a father-daughter road trip to see Grandpa. We enjoyed a great drive in my lifted Jeep I had built up for rock crawling when I lived in California. (Rock crawling is basically driving over the mountains on what can barely be considered a trail.) When we got to Grandpa's house, we settled in for a few days of fun.

Now, you have to understand that even at 81 years old, my dad had more energy than I did and was still working in his salvage yard/used car lot ten hours a day. All my life, if you wanted to spend quality time with Dad, you go over to the junkyard and work together. It's really a lot of fun!

I was helping Dad with some projects and Erin was running around looking at all the old cars having a great time. After a while, she came back, excitedly telling me she had found an emblem on the side of a truck that she wanted to take off and keep. Well, it turned out she had found an old '59 Ford truck. As I looked it over, I remembered how I had always wanted to fix up an old truck, ever since I was a boy helping Dad take apart old Pintos and then put them back together when he was running his auto body business.

Then I thought, the time is now! It's time for one more project with Dad. Erin and I started looking around at all the old trucks and I started dreaming about the project: resurrecting this truck while leaving all the old dents, scratches and peeling paint on the 1949 Ford truck. When we found it, it had no windows, no motor, no seat, no floorboard, no steering wheel—basically it was just an empty shell with surprisingly little rust.

I loved polishing and protecting that old truck and all its scars from years of hard work, wondering what story each dent could tell. I love things with texture, history, and a story, so it was quite natural to resurrect this truck as an heirloom and memorial to the family business which would probably not be in operation much longer. With Dad's help, the truck came to life faster than I expected, looking good with new Ward's Auto logos on the doors (distressed to match the patina)! To this day, I hold this experience and memory close to my heart.

Another hobby I've picked up in Michigan is cutting firewood and milling lumber with my chainsaw. I wish I could show you pictures of the walnut and cherry logs I have ripped lengthways into slabs and built into live-edge, chainsaw-cut furniture.

When I started building chainsaw-cut live-edge furniture, my wife reminded me that Jesus was a carpenter too—and I bet he really enjoyed it! This style of furniture takes a great deal of creativity and artistry to put various shapes and lines together into a beautiful table, bench, or bookshelf. Sometimes when I'm sculpting a piece of furniture, it feels like an almost spiritual experience, spending time with Jesus, the carpenter. I really love using the gift of creativity God gave me—it's pure joy.

I also love being out in nature: hiking, exploring, backpacking, swimming, surfing, and snow skiing just to name a few. I have found that living an active lifestyle which includes various forms of exercise is tremendously beneficial for my physical, mental, and spiritual health—in fact it's vitally important!

This is really just a little bit about me but it probably tells you a lot about how I may connect with God. I think this is a great way to start a discipling relationship with a young person—or really any person: just ask them what they love and, as Jesus and James K.A. Smith have asked, "What do you want?" These questions can give tremendous insight into how to help someone connect to Jesus.

As an adult with college-aged children, I know who I am pretty well. But one of the challenges of discipling young people is that they are still trying to discover who they are in many ways. So when you are willing to engage in discipling relationships with kids, you really have a great opportunity to guide them into finding their identity in/with Jesus and what that can mean for them as they engage the world around them. I just want to thank you in advance for giving that gift to a young person—it really is an amazing gift!

So, what does all this mean for me in my devotional life? First, I have in many ways found and accepted who I am as a person. When I was in college trying to find my way, it was the time of lots of Daniel and Revelation seminars. I attended many of these seminars, but they never really captured my imagination or attention. As a young adult, I told myself I would rather spend my time getting to know Jesus rather than trying to figure out exactly when he was coming. I figured that if I knew him, I would recognize him even if I wasn't expecting him that particular day.

For my first three years of college I was a biology and math major, and I did well, but not great. I eventually graduated with a Bachelor of Fine Arts degree instead, after figuring out I'm more right-brained than left-brained. I know that concept has been somewhat debunked, but I've found many people still use it because it is still helpful in many ways. For example, it has helped me understand why I don't always fit well in the Adventist church.

Adventism tends to be very left-brained with all the emphasis on doctrine and theology—so much so that in my experience, we lose most of our right-brained children because we don't know how to translate our faith in a way that makes sense to them. This is why I strongly encourage everyone to understand their personality type, learning styles, love languages, and anything else that can help them to understand how they learn and grow best so they can learn and grow best in their relationship with Jesus.

A short time ago, as I was teaching a class about creative devotions, I shared pictures of my old truck, live-edge furniture, and lots of sunset pictures. My story of who I am and how I connect with God seemed to help some of those students come to life. One student in particular asked if it was really okay for her to be herself because, even as a pastor, she was continually being told who she should be and what was acceptable. I said, "Yes! You need to be who Jesus created you to be. That's exactly what he wants from you!" The professor I was guest lecturing for said:

> It was impactful. You had courage to show up as who you are. Some of the students from other cultures and contexts especially needed to see that it was possible to integrate [into their ministries and devotional lives] some of their gifts/passions/hobbies they have that are similar to yours.

I was told another student said, "Such vulnerability and authenticity was exemplary. While I could tell our guest was well received, I felt as though he was sent for me personally." Another said, "I feel acceptable to God by you showing up as who you are."

Art and Faith

One of the things that helped me in my journey to find my way devotionally was teaching art at Lodi Academy in California. I completed my Bachelor of Fine Arts degree in graphic design at the University of Nebraska during the time I had fallen into the worldly party scene. Those were the days I was a bartender and bouncer and drank way too much. When God called me out of that life and into work for him, I also distanced myself from art because I had come to associate the two separately. It wasn't until almost 15 years later when I became a youth pastor in northern California that I decided to reintegrate art into my life.

The first thing I did when I got to Lodi was ask if I could sit in on the art classes so I could get to know the kids. The principal told me there was no art class and asked if I would be willing to teach one. That was the beginning of a great new chapter in my life where I eventually had all incoming first-year students sitting with me in a required art class. It was great being able to get to know all the high school kids in a fun, non-threatening environment. I also started having annual Engaging the Arts Spiritually outdoor youth church events where I set up stations for the youth to paint on canvas boards, sculpt with clay, write songs, create videos with spiritual content, and any other creative way to connect spiritually they could think of.

I love the fact that God gave distinct spiritual gifts of creative ability to the individuals who were called to create all the furniture and fabrics for the Old Testament sanctuary. When you think of that and look around at nature, it is easy to see that God is the greatest artist of all time! When I began teaching art to young people, I was so focused on teaching, I no longer had time to create physical art myself. What I always told people is that my artwork had become sculpting the lives of young people as I tried to lead them closer to Jesus.

Recently I have enjoyed the encouragement Makoto Fujimura gave me through his book, "Art + Faith: A theology of making," as he seems to have an artistic experience similar to mine in some ways. Fujimura says:

> I now consider what I do in the studio to be theological work as much as aesthetic work. I experience God, my Maker, in the studio. I am immersed in the art of creating, and I have come to understand this dimension of life as the most profound way of grasping human experience and the nature of our existence in the world. I call it the Theology of Making...[1]

He goes on to say:

> God continually commissions God's children to create. But as all good teachers do, God first creates a context for creativity. God had an educational plan for Adam and so created a "discovery zone" (not a correctional institution!) in Eden. Zones for discovery serve as foundation blocks for a human society to thrive. Our education plan involves all of our senses, our intellect, our emotions, and our empathic capacities, as well as our spiritual capacities. We

---

1 Fujimura, Makoto. "Art + Faith," Yale University Press, 2020, p. 3.

are to "love the Lord [our] God with all [our] heart and with all [our] soul and with all [our] mind" (Matthew 22:37).[2]

Fujimura also says:

> The Bible begins in Creation and ends in New Creation. Everywhere in between is the narrative of the broken people of God somehow being invited back and back again to reestablish this relationship with the Creator, and to be makers of the New, as heirs to the greater reality that this God is all about.[3]

To find my way devotionally, I had to understand how I communicate spiritually. I had to find my spiritual love languages and learning styles that make up the core of who I am as a person. In this way, I have found a great deal of help in structuring and nurturing my personal relationship with Jesus, and I hope you spend some time fine-tuning how you connect with God, as well. We are told that, "You will seek me and find me when you seek me with all your heart" (Jeremiah 29:13 NIV). God invites us to seek him from the heart of who we are.

What My Devotional Life Looks Like

Since I'm not a morning person; I wake up very slowly. I get up early enough that I can sit in my Amish rocker in my sunroom looking through the trees and over the lake that's in my backyard. I sit there praying, half awake. I may even drift off a bit and wake up again still talking to God. This is also part of the introverted artist in me. I sit quietly,

2 Fujimura, p. 97.
3 Fujimura, p. 150.

and even as I'm praying I don't feel like I have to do all the talking. I love sitting in silence, deliberately aware of the Holy Spirit's presence with me. The conversation may drift from how I'm feeling to what I need to accomplish to praying for my children and back around to a favorite Psalm I am in the habit of praying. This Psalm is really a check-in time for my relationship with Jesus—it helps keep me on track.

If I'm reflecting on the Old Testament sanctuary and its significance during my devotional time, I may light a small candelabra so I can visualize it better, because in many ways I'm a visual learner. Seeing those candle flames on a dark morning always reminds me that Jesus is the light of the world pointed toward by the candelabra. I'm also reminded that the oil which fed those flames in the OT sanctuary is a symbol of the Holy Spirit who can fuel me to be a light in the world for God's glory. So maybe I'll pray for those young people I'm discipling at that time too.

This type of spontaneous prayer is only one part of my devotions. I also like to settle in and read scripture, maybe a Christian book, or some other kind of cognitive nurture as well. Prayer walks are a good exercise devotionally and physically, and have great positive emotional benefits as well. When I'm in my darkest valleys, journaling prayers always helps me find my way. My journal is also full of doodling and sketching. Singing or listening to worship music can be a tremendous lift, and is a great way to start the day filled with joy as well. My goal is to be emotionally and cognitively fed in my time with Jesus each morning. And worst-case scenario—if I'm having an unusually hurried day where something unexpected has come up—I can still pray memorized scripture and talk to God in free-flowing conversation while I'm walking or driving to work or another appointment. It's not ideal, but it can still work in a pinch....

I find that starting my day filled with the Spirit from my devotional time helps me be more energetic, flexible, joyful, pleasant to be around, and definitely more productive. I'm also more open to the leading of the Spirit and where I can go on his errands. When all this is fully in place, it also gives me something to share spontaneously and organically as I have opportunities to disciple during the course of my day. I simply share some of the ways I experienced Jesus that day. Please don't get me wrong—I don't have an amazing devotional experience every day. I have highs and lows like everyone, but no matter what, I'm committed to spending the time, and even on a bad day I can still share the experiences of a day or two ago and encourage others who are struggling that better days are coming—because they always do!

The goal is to never start a day without engaging in nurturing my personal relationship with Jesus because I need that relationship in place and strong to see me through the troubled times that regularly show up in this sinful world. Offense is always the best defense.

One last thing: My morning devotional time is really just the start of the conversation with Jesus. I talk to God informally all day long; this is the application of "praying without ceasing." I try to have maybe a 5-10-minute more formal check-in during lunch, and then during the last 30 minutes before bed I try to think back over my day to see where I encountered God in special ways. At this point I tend to drift into a less formal, conversational prayer about everything that's going on. It's thinking my thoughts toward God; acknowledging he is there with me and including him in the conversation.

It's during this time at the end of my day when I frequently pick up a devotional book to read. Devotional books can be a great part of devotional life, but one page per day is never enough. There's so much more to be enjoyed with Jesus! Devotional books are often about someone else's experience with God and can be inspiring, but the end goal is to be inspired to nurture your *own* relationship with Jesus, which you can in turn share with others, inspiring them to do the same. It's your story inspiring their story as you're both immersed in his story.

Chapter 7

Stories of Devotional Lives and Styles

You have heard my story, and hopefully you saw how who I am as a person has greatly impacted how I relate to God and how I disciple others as a result. I would like to dedicate this chapter to sharing more of my students' stories, showcasing how discipleship and devotional lives can go hand in hand for them as well, with devotional life serving as the fuel for discipling others. Their stories are categorized by learning styles, with annotations regarding personality types and love languages.[1] You will find some short surveys in appendix A if you would like to see what kind of learner you are and how you relate and learn best so you can pay extra careful attention to the stories from those with similar qualities as yours. You may find some great tips to inform your own devotional life.

Here is a short, annotated index of each story so you can choose to skip to those which sound most interesting first, but I know you will eventually want to read them all. I am blessed to be able to teach students from around the world with such a variety of experiences with God and ways of connecting with him—I hope you are as inspired and informed as I am by reading them all!

---

[1] An * denotes an educated guess concerning the student's learning styles based on the story given.

VISUAL LEARNERS – DEVOTIONAL STYLE:

- Salem (visual, auditory, & tactile; sanguine-melancholic, INFP-T personality; love language: acts of service): Art was her way of escape. Her identity was questioned. All of this leads Salem to find the One who fulfills her own name's meaning. She had found her safe haven at last. "My box had space for me"

- Cristiano (visual & tactile; phlegmatic, INFJ-A personality with love language: words of affirmation): The Life of Jesus has grounded Cristiano in his study of the Bible. Through visuals and care-filled notes, he shares how he studies best, and how you can too. "I also like to learn through threads"

- Yoo-joon (visual): From a young age, Yoo-joon was destined to be around people. He has taken to the skies in a subconscious effort to draw closer to God, and through his longing to grow in devotions, he is learning to soar with Jesus. "I am still on my way to understanding and knowing God through his Gospel"

- Brendon (visual; phlegmatic, ISFJ-A personality with the love language: physical touch): Through a specific encounter as a child, Brendon has leaned into peace with God. He has now founded his walk with Jesus through a sensory-filled devotional experience, filling him with inreach essential for outreach potential. "I then felt a touch on my shoulder putting me to sleep"

AUDITORY LEARNERS – DEVOTIONAL STYLE:

- Cheng (auditory & visual; sanguine personality with love language: physical touch): From perfection to musician to devotions, Cheng travels from his experience in mainland China to his current experience with God. He has opened up the Bible and finds contentment in learning the intricacies of it. "I used to be a perfectionist"

- Anika (auditory, visual, & tactile; phlegmatic personality; love language: words of affirmation): The loss of a father, relocating twice, and living in New York City are all part of Anika's life experience. Through everything, she has learned to see the "Son's" rays through life's windows. She has embraced the lifestyle of praying without ceasing. "God was saying to me 'I have not forgotten you'"

- Leao (auditory & visual; sanguine-choleric, ENFJ-A personality with love language: quality time & words of affirmation): Suffering a brain aneurysm has not stopped Leao from choosing to see God's miraculous hand at work. He has chosen to learn even deeper truths of God through his listening abilities, and has not stopped caring about communion, fellowship, and mission. "I have the animation of a sanguine and the courage of a choleric"

- Viktor (auditory; melancholic-phlegmatic, ENFP/Protagonist personality; love language: words of affirmation & physical touch): Always wondering how to answer the toughest of life's questions, Viktor has sought the answers within the Bible, and does the classic devotion style. Having an analytical mind has helped him unpack the Bible with a deeper appreciation for theology. "'Wait, what?! What is the devil's number doing in the Bible?'"

- Pedro (auditory & kinesthetic; sanguine, ESFP-A personality with love language: physical touch & quality time): His mission year in Majuro provided significant growth to Pedro's devotional life. Thanks to the gifts of music, atmosphere, and prayer, he is able to connect with God even more fully. "At the core, behind every music I am a part of, is a gratefulness I can't fully express in words"

- Aung (auditory & tactile*): Aung found a blessing in the refugee camp. Here he shares how he became a Seventh-day Adventist, and how he has not stopped teaching and preaching about God's grace. "Being like Jesus is the loudest sermon anyone can witness"

TACTILE LEARNERS – DEVOTIONAL STYLE:

- Japheth (kinesthetic, visual, & tactile; sanguine, ENFP personality with love language: quality time & physical touch): His car was his escape— a safe place to be with God. Japheth shares how his active personality was channeled through his car escape, and eventually through his writing practice. "My devotional plan has always reflected what my faith is based on"

- Jovan (tactile*): Reading through the whole Bible can seem challenging, but Jovan shares how he reads the whole Bible at his own pace. Journaling scripture passages and prayer have kept him connected with God daily. "Yes, I set a time and place, but when I rise up from that place, I don't set God down"

KINESTHETIC LEARNERS – DEVOTIONAL STYLE:

- Enrique (kinesthetic*): Not just once, but twice, was the answer to prayer. But the second time was the real life changer for Enrique, as he learns what prayer should really be about. Since that experience, he has grown his devotional life to include intentional Bible readings, highlighting the verses that build his experience of God's restorative power. "My prayer changed immediately"

- Christopher (visual & kinesthetic; melancholic personality with love language: quality time): Construction and drumming—two kinesthetic outlets for Christopher to use as he draws closer to God during his devotions. He has found that hourly connecting with God keeps this lifestyle focused continually. "I found that every time I did woodwork, I had some kind of peace of mind"

- Allen (kinesthetic, tactile, and auditory; sanguine personality with love language: quality time & acts of service): Reflecting on verses and sitting in quietude has helped this police officer find his respite in God. Allen's motorbike experience has also given him a new perspective on his relationship with God. "As long as I fix my eyes steadily on where I want to go, I turn toward that direction"

- Alexander (kinesthetic & visual; phlegmatic personality with love language: quality time & physical touch): To read was the bane of his existence, until he opened up a book and read about the desire of the ages. This led Alexander to seek out his grandfather for Bible studies, and since then, he has found solace in reading books that bring him closer to Christ. He has also found creative outlets to continue growing his devotional walk. "My grandfather left that with me"

Visual Learners:

SALEM

My name reflects my family history and culture. My mother is Panamanian, and my father is African American Chinese. In Hispanic culture, it is normal practice to give a child more than one or two last names. It is kind of a way of keeping a family record. I was given my mother's last name and my father's last name Poon (which means Pride). My first name is Arabic, which means Peace.

Though there were some bright spots, childhood is not something I often reminisce on. It was not easy. And because there was so much need, I was often neglected. So I found ways to escape the world around me. I loved art, in all forms; music, dance, literature, and illustration were my dearest friends.

Another one of those ways of escape was imagination. I can remember digging time capsules in the backyard and making cardboard cities under the porch. I came to enjoy my cardboard home over our actual house. It was quiet there, and with my trusty dusty pack of crayola crayons, I could decorate anyway I liked. **My box had space for me.**

As I got older, I continued looking for spaces that had room for people like me. Growing up I struggled quite a bit with my identity; I would tell others who I was and so often, I was asked to prove it. I couldn't speak Spanish fluently—in fact at times I couldn't tell it apart from English. I had no accent or stereotypical features that would scream Asian. My hair was long, coarse, and curly, and my skin a mocha brown. I felt like I was not black enough nor Hispanic enough.

Yet I found my identity in Christ at a young age. It was the only place I felt fully accepted, understood, and loved. I didn't have to explain who I was to Jesus. In him, I experienced the peace I never felt at home. He was like my cardboard box. At seven years old, I was taking notes during the church service, and around this time I was also baptized. I was fascinated with God.

My love language is quality time. Perhaps this is also why I loved Sabbaths so much—a time once a week where everyone comes together. Much of what I incorporate in my devotional time are things which have given me comfort from childhood. Ideally, I have my devotional time at night as the last thing I do before closing my eyes to sleep. I go to my room, turn off the main light, and plug in my warm string of lights. I turn on my scented wax warmer and get comfy. If I am by a window and the sky is clear, especially on days when the moon is out, I open the curtains. Pencil and journal in hand, I pray and ask the Holy Spirit to fill me and help me to hear Him. Then I choose one of the following options:

- Choose a psalm or Bible story/parable (usually from the New Testament) and answer the questions: What is happening? What stood out to me? What is God's message to me?

- Choose a Bible story/parable (usually New Testament) and read it. Pray for guidance, choose a character, and reread the story. Then, rewrite the story from that character's perspective using the six senses: smell, sight, taste, touch, sound, and feel, and ask how it connects to me—what is God's message to me?

- Write a simple letter to God, expressing my thoughts and feelings in the moment, my hopes, dreams, fears, and pains, or give thanks.

Lately I have been choosing to write letters to God. I tell God about my day and whatever else is on my mind. I find this way of prayer more intimate for me. When I am not journaling, I play my guitar and I sing to God. I play and sing in a comfy spot, with my lights plugged in and, if I can, near a window.

On warmer days when I am on campus, I venture out to what I like to call my secret hideout, a small willow-like tree which no one pays much attention to. A friend of mine showed me this safe haven before she graduated. I go to this private place, and I sing and I talk to God. I feel connected to God in nature; I love the clouds, and especially panoramic views and sunsets. All of these are beautiful to me. I appreciate adding beauty and comfort to my experience with God. On days when I have no strength to pick up a guitar or a pen, I pray and meditate on the words to a song.

CRISTIANO

I didn't grow up in an Adventist home. My parents were non-practicing Catholics, and growing up, I never had a Bible-reading or family worship experience. At age 14, I started attending the local Adventist church and participated in the Pathfinder Club. I began my first experiences studying and praying alone as a teenager. At 17, I went to seminary, and at 21, I started my work as a pastor. During those teenage years, I was taught that the best way to carry out one's devotional life was to read a portion of the Bible a day, the Sabbath School lesson, and perform individual prayers. I was never taught, nor was I interested in, seeking new ways to communicate with God, and I confess that even as a pastor for 12 years, this style of devotion has changed very little in my life.

Analyzing the different learning styles and remembering my academic and spiritual experience, I can confirm that my primary learning style walks between visual and solitary. Visual learners retain information best by viewing pictures or images and respond well to colors and mind maps. In my Bible study, I love looking at the charts, lists of individuals and genealogies, and the prophetic pictures of Daniel and Revelation. **I also like to learn through threads.** Solitary or intrapersonal learners work best alone. Making notes and reciting them back are useful activities when studying by yourself. That description is made for me. Whenever I can choose between doing an activity alone or in a group, I will choose to be alone. Maybe it sounds a little antisocial, but in my experience, it's in those solitary moments when I have the best insights and experiences with God.

Although those two styles above define me, I will say that through the exercise of experimenting with new styles of devotion I have seen it is possible to get out of the routine I described above and try new experiences with music and videos, using the senses and even moments in a group to communicate with God. I have tried to include them to make my devotional plan a little more balanced.

My current devotional plan follows a four-week script and is based on the life of Jesus. During these 28 days, the common thread is focused on the life of Jesus, especially the encounters other people had with him and how their lives were transformed because of it. On each day except for Saturdays, I have two devotional moments: one in the morning and the other in the evening. Due to my preferred devotional style, the basis of study will be in readings: in the morning, parts of the Bible; and in the evening, chapters from "The Desire of Ages" by Ellen G. White.

In preparing this devotional plan, I had in mind this quote from White: "It would be well to spend a thoughtful hour each day reviewing the life of Christ from the manger to Calvary. We should take it point by point and let the imagination vividly grasp each scene, especially the closing ones of his earthly life" ("Maranatha," p. 77).

YOO-JOON

I don't have a lot of childhood memories, but I feel warm when I go back to the ones I do have. I was a child who grew up in love. When I was a baby, my mother's siblings always took care of me when my parents were busy because I cried when no one was next to me. I liked people; I liked hanging out with people. When my cognitive and communication skills developed to some extent, I would go to church with my parents. Like others, I did not know God by heart from the beginning. The Bible was unfamiliar and difficult for me, but there were many exciting things like music and friends my age, so the church, for me, was a pleasant place to meet friends.

Years later, I went to Andrews University, where I could fulfill my dream of becoming a pilot. Without knowing this was a school run by the Seventh-day Adventist Church, I chose this school based only on the aviation program.

While attending school, I naturally went back to church. At first, the door was still closed in my mind, but I gradually became disarmed and wanted to know my own God, not just in my head, not by habit, but through someone's preaching. With the help of God, I was able to graduate, but my heart was still empty, but looking back I could see all sorts of miracles had happened to me.

Knowing I had experienced many miracles which could not be achieved by power alone, I wanted to experience God physically. I listened to his voice and believed that if he could be seen in any form I could recognize, I was ready to devote myself to God.

I found out there was a way to work as a mission pilot, but working in a this field held many requirements and expectations, and I hesitated to think I was someone who could help anyone. Besides, I was still searching for God.

Eventually, I applied to the MDiv program at Andrews University, believing this would allow me the opportunity to get to know God more. Indeed, as I studied, my curiosity was sated. There are many flaws in my life, but I finally began to believe I could be used where help was needed, and where miracles were required. Even now, if I have doubts or questions, I pray to God and read the Bible to get the answer.

There are several different ways I have found to connect with God. Some like to listen to church music; some like to read the Bible. Since I'm not yet ready to fully live my devotional life, Bible study is the best. **I am still on my way to understanding and knowing God through his Gospel.** If there is an opportunity, I want to use my knowledge and faith to help others who are in remote areas, especially those who are unable to experience God's Word for themselves.

I feel refreshed when I drink coffee in the morning. So, at the beginning of each day, I read the Bible while drinking coffee. I also sometimes light candles during these activities, which helps me focus and concentrate better. It gets me in the stage of preparation.

My pursuit of a devotional life has not yet been fully established, but the direction I'm pursuing is clear: I want my faith to be firmly built up without a scratch. My current devotional time is the process of knowing and filling the hole in my faith itself. I have discovered that to start my day, I have to read a Christian book to strengthen my connection with God. And coffee is a catalyst to improve my concentration.

Ending the day with prayer is also part of my devotional life. By doing this, I feel like I'm living in the time God has allowed me to. I feel that he is with me in the good things that have happened to me, and he is happy we are planning together. I believe that even if misfortune comes to me, it will eventually be solved.

My next goal is to have more active devotional time. I believe that if you spend every moment possible developing your devotional life, it will become your lifestyle.

BRENDON

I am a person that isn't the life of a party; I tend to be the calm person in the bunch. Though I engage in conversation, I'm rarely the loudest in the room. Although my mom is charismatic and my dad a risk-taker, I am neither of those things. I'm more of the reserved, somewhat introverted type—a phlegmatic. I like to be agreeable, calm, not stepping on anyone's toes, and I like to spend time on my own.

Ever since I was a child, I have loved receiving physical affection. Although it may be uncomfortable sometimes, the most meaningful interactions between my loved ones and I come with physical touch. Proof of how much I value this love language is the story of my encounter with the divine as a child.

When I was six, I had an encounter with either God or an angel. Though I'm not entirely sure which, it was surely one of the two. My dad laid me in bed, kissed me, and turned off the lights of my room. As I was falling asleep, I remember feeling someone else in the room, but no one was there. **I then felt a touch on my shoulder putting me to sleep.** Even to this day, I've never felt such peace as I did in that moment. God sent me to sleep with his peaceful, comforting touch. I'm not clingy but I appreciate personal time with him, and when I spend more time with God—reading the Bible, praying, and singing—things just get better.

I have never been much of a candle person, but I decided to try incorporating it into my devotional practice, and it did much to ingrain the devotional experience in my memory. For example, there was an evening when I did a mini communion for myself. I enjoyed it very much when I lit up the candle, had grape juice and crackers, and wrote in my journal. It was quality time with God that I appreciated. If anything, this experience with God was much better since I commemorated the victory that remains forever.

I love the reflection periods in my devotionals. Reflecting on the text leads me to imagine the biblical scenes, behold the glory of God with Moses, decide what I want to talk to God about, and pray like the heroes of faith did. Reflection sets my mind on God as I encounter him in our time together. Reflection didn't allow me to read and forget; rather, I read, imagined, contemplated, beheld, and worshiped.

Another act of my devotional life which is significant to me is outreach. I went out into my neighborhood seeking people to talk to and pray for. It was a blessing for me to put into practice the things which I was learning in my devotionals and personal sessions with God. As I listened to the people I met and ministered to their needs, I was blessed. I even met new neighbors and they, too, were excited to meet someone new. I think that is a major blessing of outreach: encountering new people, even when they are already close in distance.

Auditory Learners:

CHENG

I used to be a perfectionist. Anything I was involved in I demanded the best. For anyone, such a burden is naturally unsustainable, so after a period of time, I would feel tired, and even my health status was showing a red flag. For a long time in the past, I approached devotional practice with this "event-oriented" way of thinking. A sentence I often used to motivate myself was, "It is better to let the oxen die from exhaustion than to overturn the oxcart." It means that in order to achieve the goal of one thing, it is necessary and worthwhile to pay a heavy price.

There were four years when I worked hard for more than thirteen hours every day, leading various meetings in the church, organizing Bible study classes, holding discipleship training camps, leading prayer meetings and spiritual revival meetings, and more. Due to my overloaded schedule, I finally fell ill one winter morning. Long-term desk work caused problems in my lumbar spine, and the sharp pain prevented me from standing and walking. Also, I was suffering from severe hemorrhoids and rectal disease. I was forced to undergo necessary surgery and spent months resting in a hospital bed.

This incident caused me to pause and think. In just a few short years, my body and mind suffered such a blow, there must be something wrong. After all, my illnesses were caused by doing "spiritual" things, not "sinful" things; why didn't God intervene? Why did God make me suffer so much? But I finally understood that, in fact, what God cares about is *relationship*. What I value is the process and its result, but God values the state of my mind and heart.

Judging from the characteristics of learning styles, I first belong to the solitary (intrapersonal) learning type. I don't like the mode of studying together in a group; sometimes it can be a kind of torture for me. I much prefer to study and think alone.

In mainland China, it is difficult for Seventh-day Adventists to find biblical experts. I had very few opportunities to receive expert guidance, which forced me to do my own independent research and exploration through various channels, and gradually apply it in practice bit by bit. This has formed my own independent learning mode.

Because of my learning styles, I naturally relate to visual and auditory stimuli. I once studied vocal music with singers from the Shanghai Conservatory of Music. I like singing and immersing myself in the melody of music, enjoying the indescribable physical and mental relaxation brought by music. Music brings me into a deep inner silence, focuses my thoughts, allows for deep thinking, and stimulates my inspiration and creative thinking. To clarify, the music I'm talking about here refers to genres like nocturnes or lyric hymns. Along with pictures, props, drama, or other art forms, I am receptive to information conveyed by words and language.

To incorporate this into my study of the Bible, I read the scriptures aloud chapter by chapter, and then read aloud the analysis and explanation of the scriptures written by Ellen

White. This forms a deep memory of what I have learned. I keep several thick notebooks full of insights I have gleaned during my study. Therefore, the best way for me to absorb information is to simultaneously see with my eyes, listen with my ears, and record with my hands.

I go through each devotional in six steps. The first step is to pray: I ask the blood of Jesus to cleanse me so my spirit and whole being can rejoice before God. The second step is to worship: I praise God and thank him through songs or heart worship. The third step is to listen: by reading or listening to God's words, I can enter the way of truth, see the practical teachings, and then gain the spiritual principles and order God has given me. The fourth step is to meditate: following the inspiration of the Holy Spirit, I will think about God's nature, and understand his will according to God's words, and turn to his provision and guidance in personal matters. The fifth step is to compare: I will follow God's light to conduct deep self-examination, be humble and self-cleaning, and deal seriously with various life problems. The sixth and final step is to respond: based on my devotional, I respond to God's revelation and guidance in my prayer, and ask for the help of the Holy Spirit to implement what I have heard into my life.

ANIKA

My world fell apart when I was only eleven years old, after my dad sustained fatal injuries in a car collision. There was no stability in my life after he passed. Before I was able to finish high school, I had to relocate (unwillingly) to New York City—alone—where I resided with an abusive cousin. Despite this, I was a straight-A student with scholarships to Columbia University, PENN State, Stony Brook University, and NYU. Due to jealousy of my academic success, I was no longer welcome in my cousin's home, so, at age 16, I moved to Florida to be with my sister, who had just had her second son. I became the live-in nanny and maid. All of my scholarships disappeared after relocating, and my sister would not let me leave as I was the only source of help for her new family. I then completed college in three years and returned to New York to be on my own.

How does this affect my devotion? After retaining a therapist, I had to find the connection between my past experiences distrusting family (especially my mother) and, ultimately, my distrust in God. I loved God with all my heart, yet being a fourth generation Adventist suddenly meant nothing. I had to acknowledge the fact that I was angry with God.

There were moments when I had no food, I was homeless, I had no support from my family, I was depressed and suicidal; I was angry with God. There were days when I was so impoverished, yet I would still faithfully walk several miles to church every Sabbath and then walk the miles back home. I did not expect to serve the Lord and still be in such dire need. I was angry with God. Yet still, in one of those bitter, harsh, cruel moments in life, when I broke down sobbing at Grand Central Station, I heard the voice of God speaking to me. From that moment, I learned to know his voice, and I now love hearing his voice.

Praying, for me, is such a passionate, intimate time with God. I love praying and I began my prayer walk with God in Queens, New York City. I would walk around in circles in my little basement apartment singing, then reading the Psalms out loud, and becoming comfortable praying and hearing my own voice in prayer. The most special moments to me are where when I heard God respond to me. I always like to think he was patiently waiting on me. In truth, praying saved me.

I was about to commit suicide one night. I lived in a basement in Queens, with no natural light entering the apartment. My landlords were not leaving me without sunlight deliberately; they were just doing what normal homeowners do—using every inch of space for storage, thus blocking the only window to natural light. That night, moments before I was successful, I felt the peace of God enter my room. I was hysterically crying. I knew what I was about to do was wrong, and when I felt the presence of God, I felt so ashamed. I prayed and spoke with God that night until morning and for the first time, I saw the sun's rays peeking through my little kitchen window. **God was saying to me, "I have not forgotten you."**

Now, I am normally awake by 2:30 or 3 a.m. each day for my devotions. I pray with my prayer partner on the phone or by myself, and if I am praying by myself, my husband may join me. My sole purpose for waking up at 3 a.m. is to pray and talk with God. I pray again at 6 a.m. after my husband leaves, and I often read scripture. I try to make it the very first thing I do every day. I make sure to be fully present, leaving my phone in the bedroom and going to my prayer corner in the living/dining room. I sometimes sing, but usually it's hymns sung in my amazingly raspy morning voice.

I think by now I've embodied that Bible verse, 'Pray without ceasing.' I love the Lord, I love talking to him, and I love when he speaks back to me—in the scriptures, in a song, or when I hear his voice. Make room for the Lord; he will make room for you.

LEAO

Who am I? I am a versatile and easily adaptable person. I quickly get involved with people and value harmony in the environment. I like to talk to people, and I have good communication skills—I consider what my words will do to people, and I care about their emotions. I have a strong tendency toward immediate action, and I value rules and traditions, which leads me to be committed to my ideals and principles.

I tend to live cautiously, avoiding risks. I seek to follow processes and procedures, paying attention to details concertedly. I seek the support of people I trust to validate my decisions. I am socially oriented and naturally seek to make friends with people. I seek harmony and acceptance, preferring to share findings and opinions with people and avoiding conflicts. I have a certain anxiety about being able to meet the expectations I make for myself.

I'm concerned about doing everything right the first time. To accomplish that, I wait and look for the norms and rules surrounding what I need to do. I can make and carry out projects quickly and correctly, and I check everything throughout the process. I try to absorb the stress of everyday life, taking advantage of the full potential of my behavioral characteristics. I react strongly to environmental stimuli, which allows me to make changes and adaptations in my life to carry out my daily activities and still be willing to perform more tasks or activities.

I have the animation of a sanguine and the courage of a choleric. It is the most outgoing and decisive of all the combinations, as both temperaments are extroverted. Also, quality time is my love language; I feel truly loved when I spend time with the people I care about. I also feel love through words of affirmation. My learning style is auditory, as I prefer to listen to lectures and podcasts. In addition to listening, I enjoy reading aloud and participating in debates. I learn a lot from the conversations. To memorize, I usually speak, ask, and repeat information. I am also a relational worshiper. My experience with God is connected with church members and with feelings and personal reflections on God, and I like to think of new ways to praise God actively and practically where I can feel his presence.

I have always been involved in church activities, and since I was a child, I desired to be a pastor and tell people about the love of Jesus. I am grateful that God preserved my life when I suffered a brain aneurysm when I was six years old. God performed a miracle in my life by allowing blood clotted in the cerebellum to leave my brain for no explainable scientific reason. I was grateful for this miracle God performed in my life, and, emboldened, I asked for a brother to be born on the same date I was healed. A year later, my brother was born naturally on that same date.

I know God works great miracles and cares about the simplest requests we make. I know he has called me to meet needs and invite people to turn from sin and be reconciled to him.

Where am I? Today, I am striving to have a deep relationship with God, despite sometimes failing and prioritizing other things over him. I realize that sometimes, because I'm too busy sorting out pastoral work, I put aside my devotion to God and make the mistake of thinking that because my job is religious, I'm already developing a relationship with him. I realize I need to dedicate myself more to planning and perseverance to be a better person for my wife, my child, and God.

What do I want? I want to prioritize time with God and my family. My devotional plan is based on three pillars: communion, fellowship, and mission. Through communion, I want to be a friend of God. Through fellowship, I want to be friends with the people close to me. Through the mission, I aim to win new friends for Jesus.

VIKTOR

When I was 15 years old, I went on a Pathfinder campout. I woke up early one day and, since I had nothing else to do, I thought that I might read the Bible. I used to be one of those kids who knew all the Bible stories, and I knew Christians were supposed to read their Bibles, so it seemed like the right thing to do. So, I picked up my Bible and eventually turned to Revelation. Once there, I just flicked through the pages until something caught my attention.

Suddenly there was the number "666." I clearly remember thinking, **"Wait, what?! What is the devil's number doing in the Bible?"** Then I read the entire chapter, thinking it was meant to be taken literally. Of course, when I shared it with the people around me, luckily one of them knew a bit about Revelation and started teaching me what it actually meant.

This was what kickstarted me as a "Bible nerd." After that campout, I went home and ended up having Bible studies with my uncle. This led to me to read a chapter of the Bible each evening and then ask difficult questions of my uncle. During that time, he recommended I do my devotions in the mornings instead. It was good, but I felt like something was missing in the evening, so I started doing devotions then, too. I stayed consistent with this devotional life until I was 27. This has shown me that I like to read the Bible and pray.

I really like the classical devotion style and I do not need all the other fancy things.

In all of this time, I had a strong connection with God. There were of course ups and downs, but I could easily feel when I had forgotten a morning devotion. Then, when I graduated from engineering, I had a hard time finding a job. My days had no rhythm, which led to my devotional life suffering. Though I had gotten it somewhat back into shape by the time I started at Andrews, it was still very sporadic. This class has helped me kickstart it again, and I am very happy about that.

With all of this background, it is time to look at my specific devotional style. I really like to analyze myself, and I also enjoy analyzing things I encounter. Because of this, I have a good grasp of where I stand theologically. With this analytical mind, I really like things which stimulate the intellect. I love finding a tough dilemma to wrestle with, and enjoy when people ask me difficult questions about the Bible. Most of all, I love taking something complex and difficult and explaining it so everyone can understand.

In my devotional life, this is expressed through a love for theology. For example, I enjoy hearing a sermon which describes complex problems and explains them in an understandable way. I often think about how I can rephrase what I've learned so it is even easier to understand. I love to read the Bible and ask the hard questions, and then use the Bible to solve them. I feel closest to God when I talk about him and help others understand him better.

Since I am geared toward the more logical side, I yearn to simply go into the depth of God's word and not take the time to heat water for a hot drink. Trying this addition to my devotional time has taught me that it may help others, but it is not my style of devotions.

Something I have realized, though, is that I may need to slow down. I normally do this by going for a walk, particularly to prepare for a sermon, or when many things are pressing down on me. This allows me to stop, refocus on God, and put everything in order. I will be more intentional with these breaks now.

I also realized that I cannot do the "sit and wait" prayer thing. My mind never stops. When God talks to me, it is often through the way my thoughts wander during prayer. Most often that is a bad thing, but I have experienced revelations I needed for a sermon or a tough problem in this way. I guess that is my version of just sitting still and waiting. I cannot do that on command, but I guess those who "sit and wait" don't always hear something, either.

Through this experience, I have realized how much I love my own devotional life as it is. All I needed was to get it restarted.

PEDRO

The first step I would consider sharing with someone trying to start this life is the same step I took when starting my own devotional life: find out what does work for you, and what doesn't. Give each effort your fullest attention, with no distractions in the way. You probably know the first distraction I am going to mention: the smartphone. It shouldn't be anywhere near your devotional space or time. Then, think about your favorite relationship in life. How much time do you spend with that person? Is it a friendship? A marriage? A parent or sibling? How do you nurture that relationship? What are your favorite things to do with that person? Imagine starting your devotional life by doing pottery with God! Or writing a poem about how God makes you feel. Or arranging a space in which you think the

Holy Spirit would enjoy being. Prayer and scripture-reading would be the bare minimum to keep consistent while other activities relating to devotional life could change.

I was raised Adventist by two parents who were both relatively new to the faith. I'd say they had very conservative mindsets when it came to religion, and this affected my views during the earlier stages of my life. I attended Adventist academy from kindergarten through eighth grade, and then left to start a public school/homeschool hybrid called charter school. A self-paced and semi-classroom type of learning was interesting to say the least. After two years of that, I started attending a normal day-to-day public high school. It was then that I started to "wake up" to my faith.

After public high school, I was in a nebulous space concerning my next step, so I reluctantly took my father's advice and decided to attend Walla Walla University. There, my life started to take small turns for the worse. My integrity waned, my life choices were not healthy, and I stopped attending church. Two years went by with less and less God in my life. It was the summer of 2013 when I received an email that changed my life.

The email asked for desperate/urgent help regarding student mission work in the Marshall Islands. I answered and, long story short, I raised $4,300 in a few months and then found myself on a plane to the island of Majuro. This is where my spiritual life began to really take shape, as I didn't have anything else to rely upon. The internet didn't allow for the old connections I had back home to grow, so I had to build new ones, and the biggest one was with Jesus. I spent two years of my life on that island, and my devotional life started developing and finding a firm foundation here.

One of the biggest reasons I remain Adventist to this day is music, an art form which is directly linked to my devotional life. Part of my everyday walk is singing and playing to God. I also write songs and share them with others in hopes that these songs can inspire worship. Music is a spiritual gift God has manifested in my life, and it will continue to be my passion until my last day. **At the core, behind every piece of music of which I am a part is a gratitude I can't fully express in words.**

I thank God so much for instilling this beauty in my heart and soul; I have dedicated all I do musically to him and any success I find will have the same dedication. I think it is important in anyone's spiritual walk to find a gift they can share with others which can be cultivated in their personal time of devotion. I imagine God hears my music and delights in it. I imagine he is singing along with me and guiding melodies I choose for songs about him or about others.

Let me now share some of the ways I have found work well in my devotional life with God. First is the atmosphere of the room where I spend time with Him. I like to keep the space clean, removing any distractions (especially technology), and making sure I have plenty of time so I am not rushed. Then, I create an ambience by lighting a candle, which I snuff out when I am done. It is a symbol that my time with God is active and alive. Fire isn't stagnant; it moves and it can grow.

Second is the musical experience: listening or playing music is how I start my devotional time. If I am singing, I usually pick a spot in scripture and think of a few different song ideas based on what I think God wants to say to me through the words of the Bible. Then I can pick worship songs that have to do with the themes I chose, or are directly inspired from the verses I happen to be looking through. I have found it best not to limit where in the Bible I read.

Third is prayer time. This may or may not have some music attached to it. Often it is just me speaking to God, sometimes about myself or about people I care about. I spend most of my time in this portion of my devotions.

AUNG

I was born and raised in what is now called Myanmar (formerly Burma), a country in Asia. The Chin state, where I lived, was one of the poorest states in the country. Unfortunately, my dad passed away when I was seven. My mom tried her best to keep my family prospering; she raised goats, and I always helped her sell their milk.

My mom really wanted me to be educated, so I was sent to Yangon, which used to be the capital city, for school. There I lived in a boys' hostel and life was tough. To make my story short, I ended up spending more than ten years living in a refugee camp in Thailand.

In general, living in a refugee camp is usually considered a bad situation, but for me, it was one of the biggest blessings, because it was at this refugee camp where I became a Seventh-day Adventist. From that time on, I was involved in service, teaching the youth Sabbath School class, singing songs, and preaching.

At first, I wanted to be a singer. I sang for weddings and even released a mini gospel album. However, I found myself becoming more of a preacher than a singer.

Through these experiences, I have learned that I am the type of person who wants to worship freely without stress and anxiety. I am a very practical person. I feel very strongly that God is worthy to be praised with all my heart, strength, and mind. I really like Psalm 34:8, which emphasizes praising

God because of the blessings of trusting in him. I also love singing and preaching, and I like clapping to give the glory to God. I am very interested in engaging with the audience/congregation. As an evangelist, I always hunger to preach and share the love of God with others.

Being like Jesus is the loudest sermon anyone can witness. Living like God is not only a choice in a moment, but a continual lifestyle; it is a life-long process. I also believe that having a devotional plan is very important, and will help keep me disciplined to maintain this daily walk with God.

Tactile Learners:

JAPHETH

I am an active person, and always have been, so being locked in the house, following a weekly routine of the same activities was killing me inside. Nevertheless, I was never one to speak up about anything, so I suffered in silence. My breakthrough happened when I got my first car: a 2006 blue Honda Civic. Whenever I was in the car, I began to open my heart up to God. I had years' worth of emotions and thoughts finally pour out when I was in my car.

This car was my safe place and thanks to that Honda Civic, I became a car enthusiast. I started looking at turbo kits, mufflers, window tints, and other DIY projects online which allowed me to realize my passion for working with my hands to create. This passion was later enhanced when my family moved to Texas and I began working in construction to pay for school while studying theology at Oakwood University. In that three-year period, I discovered a talent for arts and crafts as I made origami figures and drawings to give away to a girl I was interested in—and it worked!

However, there were other moments where sorrow and pain were abundant in my life. One such moment was when I had a terrible car accident which caused me to lose an entire year in college. I had lost my safe place (my first car) and was doubtful of the reason behind this event in my life. However, God is a master at making beauty out of crisis, and because of this event, I learned that I also love writing. In those moments of apparent destruction of dreams and hopes, God used all my emotions to inspire me to write some of the sincerest prayers I have ever made to God. When my mouth cannot utter what my heart is experiencing, my hand and a pen can make my heart become real on a sheet of paper.

My devotional plan has always reflected what my faith is based on. Coming from a background of being restricted in many ways—including how to communicate with God and how to have a connection with him—most of my relationships were superficial. It was hard for me to seek further and think outside the box. Thus, my attempts at relating to God were superficial, too.

I used to pray, read a chapter in the Bible, and finish with prayer, but it never filled me, so I never kept up with my reading. It wasn't until I began the MDiv program when I discovered life is rather colorful and beautiful because God created it that way.

Confession was absolutely crucial in my process of learning how to relate to God in a genuine and open way, as it did away with my shame and fear of being judged and condemned just for being who I am. At the end of the day, however, God wants me to come to him as I am, and that became more real to me as I walked through this course.

JOVAN

I grew up in Haiti, and my family barely knew who God was. Somehow, I ended up at the seminary after some years of attending church, and I decided to follow the path to become a pastor. There are a few simple things I've learned in my life which help me stay on track with my devotion to God; getting close to God is not about a reading plan, a calendar, a set of rituals, or even a prayer closet. It is all about a devoted heart. So, while these tips to develop daily devotions might help me invest in habits for intentional time with God, habits cannot replace a personal relationship with him.

I often hear from people who say they just can't seem to hear God. God is clear in his Word that if we seek him, we will find him. He is not playing hide-and-seek with us; he wants to hear from us and wants us to hear from him. When I enter into devotional time, I choose to be open to his voice and direction. I challenge myself to go through a reading plan which leads me through the entire Bible, but I do not want to get caught in the trap of getting behind and then giving up altogether—I go at a pace that works for me.

One thing I love to do is journal scripture. I choose at least one verse every day from my reading and write it down. Then I write my prayer down, too. This keeps me engaged and gives me a record to go back to on days when my prayers are lacking and my thoughts are wandering.

Daily devotion is more about loving God and developing a relationship with him than developing a schedule. Daily discipline and a plan help tremendously. Get to know God by praying and getting into his Word.

This is what devotion looks like to me. It's less about following a set of rules, regulations, or list of reading prompts, and more about letting God into every moment of my life. Rather than thinking of devotions with God as a one-time a-day thing, I consider it an all-day thing. **Yes, I set a time and place, but when I rise up from that place, I don't set God down.** He goes with me. Remembering he is with me is when my daily devotion is taken to the next level. Acknowledging his presence regularly throughout the day is why some people seem to have more of God than others. It's not that they somehow have a higher dose of Jesus; they just seek him more and therefore find him more.

Kinesthetic Learners:

ENRIQUE

Experiencing God through prayer and joyful praise in personal devotion is akin to receiving a breath of fresh air daily. The very act of intentionally setting aside time to experience the presence of God should become as second nature to us as is the act of breathing.

When I was nine years old, my mother was deathly ill. After medical tests and procedures, she was diagnosed with colon cancer and was told the cancer had spread quickly and she only had a few months to live. I remember my mother and father having a tearful conversation with my siblings and I about how Mommy would no longer be with us after a few months, but also telling us that God was so powerful he could heal her in an instant.

As the days went on, the doctors reached out to try a procedure in hopes of lengthening my mother's life expectancy. The entire church was in intensive prayer day and night. When my mother went in for a final examination, the doctors were shocked and amazed: there was no trace of cancer in her body! At nine years old, I learned I serve a powerful God who loves and is eager to listen to our prayers.

I wish I could say that from then on, I have intentionally searched for God on a daily basis, but the truth is, I slid out of this lifestyle. Later, as a 22-year-old still living at home, I noticed my mother begin to get sick again. I immediately resolved I would take a proactive approach and search for God immediately. I began waking up at 4 a.m., spending time in Bible study and prayer specifically and exclusively for my mother.

As I was going through this time of strengthening my relationship with God, I began to pray fervently for one million dollars, an amount I believed to be sufficient to get my mother adequate medical attention. I was so serious about this that I even began to be very specific: "God, if you love me and my mom, would you please provide me with one million dollars in a UPS truck delivery." Back then, receiving a package from a delivery truck was uncommon for my family; it was my way of "throwing out the fleece."

After about a month of fervent prayer, I noticed a UPS truck driving up our driveway. I immediately bolted to the truck. As I approached the driver with joy, thinking my prayers had been answered, my joy quickly turned to grief. The UPS driver was simply lost and looking for another address.

I went inside and prayed, "Why God? Why would you play this cruel joke on me?" As I was praying, a thought pierced through my mind, and I felt God answer, "Why are you asking for a million dollars to heal your mother instead of asking me to heal her?"

My heart was torn. **My prayer changed immediately.**

It's been 14 years and by God's grace, my mother still enjoys good health. For 14 years, I've been praying for his will to be done and never mine. I have made spending time with God as second nature as breathing. Scripture says, "You will seek me and find me when you seek me with all your heart" (Jeremiah 29:13).

Although I have always been a morning person, I find that nighttime is when most I enjoy sitting and reflecting on God's promises in prayer. Spending time with God in the night is when I can experience the conversation aspect of devotional life. Now, starting off the day with God is always important, so in the morning I will often sing praises to God with my guitar and feed on his word. Going through one chapter a day, I highlight words or phrases which capture my attention. I'll often meditate on it for a while and ask God to speak to me throughout the day. Then, as I go through my day, I think constantly about the verses I read in the morning, and wait on God to reply.

Another aspect of my devotional life is including God in the things I love to do. I used to be a contractor, so I love to build and make things with my hands. Recently, I built a barn-style shed out of reclaimed wood and metal sheets I got from my neighbor's old chicken house. By including God in my hobby, I was able to experience God's restorative power in a sinner's life. As I was pulling out nails from old lumber and repainting the metal, I could hear God telling me that no matter what I've been through, and in what shape I am in, he can and will still use me for his honor and glory.

I enjoy using my hands to praise God, lighting candles at night as I pray, and even breaking challah bread with my family as we bring in the Sabbath. All these things give my devotional life a more tangible experience which engages the mind in a whole new way. When I engage all of my senses in worshiping and praising God through daily devotion, I feel I am truly seeking God with all of my heart.

CHRISTOPHER

While here in America, I picked up construction as my hustle to survive. (I had taken an industrial arts class in high school.) **I found that every time I did woodwork, I had some kind of peace of mind.** It was not intimidating to try to figure out an angle to cut or work on a challenging project; rather, I found it was quite therapeutic.

Growing up, I also had a love for music and was surrounded and nurtured by musicians. I loved playing the drums, and I do consider myself a musician because music has been a big part of my life. Back home, singing was a way of celebrating, mourning, expressing oneself, etc. When I am saddened, I pick up my guitar and start picking away and just humming a random song. But I notice when I sing as a performance, I don't get the same feeling I get as when I am by myself just picking the guitar or playing piano in the silence and isolation. Sometimes it feels like when I do it for people, it takes away the authenticity—the organic nature—it has when I am by myself.

So, how do my heart, construction, and music relate to my devotional life? There's a reason I picked up construction (besides the financial help it gives). There's a reason God also gifted me with music. These all play a big part in my search to connect with God. When I am engaged in these activities, I feel close to God. Additionally, since I grew up on an island, I have always had a special relationship with nature, and I have seen how nature has proven the words of the Psalmist: nature is God's choir that sings his praises.

I tend to do devotions in the morning at 3 a.m., when everything is still quiet and distractions are minimum. I sit in my living room on my recliner, reading through my devotional (it is a practice now for me to use "My Utmost For His Highest" by Oswald Chambers), then I close it and meditate, asking myself where I am in my relationship with God in relation to what I have read. I recently installed recessed lights in my living room with a dimmer switch, which gives a warm lighting atmosphere while I am doing my reading.

Throughout my day, I look for ways to remain in connection with God. One way I do this is by setting my watch to signal each hour with a vibration so I can redirect my mind toward God. I usually send up a prayer request or praise to God or listen to a song or sing while meditating. I also try to have special times with God through projects. I find little wood projects to work on and, during this, I find myself engaged with God. I imagine God in the room, beside me as I am measuring. I imagine Jesus working with Joseph as a carpenter, and I relate this to my relationship with God. Additionally, raising my children has taught me a lot more about God than I understood as a single man; it also has also directed my mind to pray over and for them in my time with God.

ALLEN

Relationships, healthy ones, require intentionality and effort. With the understanding that our relationship with God is not excluded, it is important for me to be conscious of the role I play in the communion and growing journey I experience with God.

We are blessed through the reconciled work of the Father through the sacrifice of Jesus to have this opportunity to be intimate with God. Engaging in this requires that I first acknowledge the privilege given to me in having this restoration, and secondly, as God has moved toward me in love, I must also move toward him. In light of this, I find myself spending time with God devotionally in stillness, reflecting on a text or listening to gospel music. I try to see Jesus in the text I'm reading, especially if it's not the gospels, and I like to reflect and sit in quietness and engage in gratitude practices.

Born in the inner city of New York, I grew up with my two brothers and my parents in our single-bedroom apartment. Most of my childhood years were spent playing with the other kids in my neighborhood and in Pathfinders at church. I lost my baby brother due to medical problems as a child, and because my godparents were bringing me to church at the time, it caused me to pray, as I desired God to resurrect my brother.

As time continued and I started to grow in reading the Word, my relationship with God grew as well. When I became a police officer, my prayer life grew even more, as I took into account the present danger I confronted on a daily basis; I never know, ultimately, what my shift will look like and if I will even return home to my loved ones.

My hobbies and interests through which I see the Holy Spirit moving are working out, and riding my motorcycle. While I work out and endure the pain that brings about growth, I receive support from texts like Psalm 30:5, which states that joy comes in the morning after weeping. Although I will endure something for the present moment, I know that in the end, something greater will come about in me. This also reminds me of 2 Corinthians 4:16-17.

When I ride my motorcycle, unity constantly comes to mind. The more I ride, the more in tune I feel with the bike, and I have learned that even my body weight can throw things off. There is a need for me to be mindful of my terrain and how it can affect how I travel, and mentally how I navigate life. I remember struggling trying to learn how to turn the bike while I was taking the class to get my license; the guidance given to me by the instructor was to look in the direction I desired to go, and my body would follow. Sure enough, it has proven true: **as long as I fix my eyes steadily on where I want to go, I turn toward that direction.** This rings true for my walk with God, too.

ALEXANDER

A good portion of my childhood was spent either drawing or building something. I hated reading; I didn't want to sit still. I wanted to just play outside or draw or build something. My disdain for reading didn't last; in fact, God was the one who brought about that change.

One night, I had a dream where God showed me how my life was going, and he convicted me of my need for Jesus. I gave my life to him that night and decided to read my Bible the next morning. I did—and it was so confusing! I still read it, though, because I knew that's where I was supposed to learn of Jesus. Again, try to imagine a child who hates reading, reading a book—not just any book, but the Bible.

When I couldn't understand the Bible, I turned to "The Desire of Ages" by Ellen White. But when I opened that book in my grandfather's library and saw 800+ pages, I said "NOPE," and put it back. I found another book called "The Messiah," a 400-page adaptation of "The Desire of Ages," so I read that. When I finished, I was absolutely amazed and felt accomplished because this was a big book for me! More importantly though, I grew to love and desire more of Jesus. That book opened my eyes to what he did for me, and the Bible began to be precious in my eyes. I then decided to read "The Desire of Ages," and I can say that it is simply the greatest book on the life of Jesus Christ apart from the scriptures.

During this phase of my life, much time was spent simply reading and being in God's presence. I felt so unworthy and overwhelmed by how much Jesus loved me. It's a time in my life I will never forget.

I really wanted to get to know Jesus more, but I had a lot of questions. Who would I go to? As it turns out, my grandfather, Eldon, always tried to get his grandkids to read their Bibles and always talked about Jesus. I went to my grandfather for help, and we had many Bible studies. This was how I developed a really close relationship with my grandfather. He was the first person to lead me closer to Jesus. He was the first person I opened up to about what Jesus did for me in that dream. I became the first and only of his grandchildren to go into ministry. My grandfather has been dead now for a few years, but that time with him has influenced how I spend time with Jesus today.

I must be totally honest: although I enjoy doing things with my hands like carpentry or drawing, what I primarily do today is read my Bible. The times when I feel closest to God have always been when I opened my Bible—**my grandfather left that with me.** But I shouldn't forget how I once enjoyed spending my time in carpentry and drawing.

Today, I tend to lean more toward information and deep Bible study, but to expand my horizons, I also try to use my creative side. I focus on a theme such as the synoptic gospels. During that time, I primarily engage with Jesus through deep study and prayer. I share what I learn with my wife and people at my church. My focus is on the mind and the heart. The structure is to read the gospels to see what the passage tells me about Jesus, then write down a conversation with Jesus.

Another theme/topic could be the Sanctuary. This one gets me excited! My plan is to spend time reading about the different aspects of the Sanctuary and then use my creative side by drawing every piece of furniture, or perhaps even using my carpentry skills to create a replica.

As I spend time with these creative outlets, I also like to listen to music. So, this time will be spent doing less in-depth study and more using my imagination, reflecting on the experience of the sanctuary and trying to capture its beauty.

I'm the type of person who, when something captures my attention, I am locked in. I don't want to do anything else. It becomes an obsession and that's all I want to do. So, having my devotions scheduled into the day for only a short time frame is tough. When I draw, I draw for hours and I don't want to stop. Knowing myself, I plan for most of my devotionals to be in the evening. I aim to spend at least a half hour with him every day.

Chapter 8

Sarah's Story and Devotional Life

CHILDHOOD

I was raised on the Front Range of Denver, Colorado. That mountain range witnessed the painful times my family went through during my childhood and adolescent years.

Neither my mom nor my dad had healed from, nor processed, their own childhood traumas. They were still broken when they were married, and this showed as they tried to parent three small children. I am the oldest of three, with a younger sister and a younger brother. Despite the few years my dad felt a calling from God and tried to be a Christian, he was called again and again to the wasting grounds of drugs, women, and recklessness. He would host parties in our basement and the smell of marijuana would fill our house, along with other scents I have never identified. Young women would parade themselves through our living room as my mom sat on the couch with me and my siblings, and act as though they owned my dad and belonged in our home. It made me feel a strong and strange sense of jealousy for my mom. I wished—always wished—that my dad could swoon for my mom as he did for these young women who partied with him in the basement.

Out of a sense of responsibility, my dad painted houses for a meager living. Out of the passion of his heart, he raced cars. But when he began to have grand mal seizures when I was 11, it led to his necessary abandonment of racing. This plunged him into further self-destructive behaviors, endlessly chasing after anything that would fill his soul, which was never found.

During this same time, my mom had a man friend move in with us. His girlfriend had recently broken up with him and he needed a place to stay. My dad pushed him to care for my mom and us three children so he could be relieved of his duties as husband and father.

My little girl heart desperately wanted to save my dad—to save my family—and I felt so powerless. I used to think of all the ways I could lavish love on him, be more beautiful than all those women, and give him the desire to be with us, but it went unnoticed.

The emotional turmoil my mother and father were experiencing blinded them to the little ones under their feet. Dad left us, and this new unwanted man took his place. This began years of constant moving from home to home and school to school, never settling down, but always having to pack again, saying goodbye to neighborhoods and friends.

Mom and this man were eventually married and were always chasing after greener grass; they were too restless to settle down for any length of time. We lived in many different homes in the suburbs of Denver, in an apartment in the city, on 40 acres of flat woodland in the middle of nowhere Colorado, in a small town in Minnesota, and back to the suburbs of Denver. By the time I graduated high school, I had attended 10 different schools. My heart and mind and soul grew restless and bitter, and I followed in my father's footsteps and entered years of self-destruction.

Alcohol and drugs, risky behaviors, a suicide attempt when I was 16, and so many careless nights and sleepy days became my normal. I held no value for myself, my life, or God; saying no to a boy didn't matter, and trying to stay positive and hopeful would plunge me into deep, depressive states I could scarcely escape from. I worked hard to make money to get through high school. I found work to be a productive space in which I could drown my sorrows, forget about my home life, and feel safe. I worked as many hours as I could to avoid home.

These behaviors and lack of self-worth bled into my eventual marriage. At work, I met a boy who was silent and obscure. He was a prolific poet, ran on the edges of society, and was attached to no one. He was a dark, witty, intelligent boy who captured me in a weird way. We were eventually married at 20 years old and had four beautiful babies together by the time we were 27. But his lust and love for beautiful women called him away. He abandoned us when our fourth baby was just over a month old.

Loss, abandonment, and tragedy took their toll, but all my efforts were centered on giving my children the best life possible. They were my everything and I deeply and fervently loved them. The love I experienced for my own children opened my heart for the Holy Spirit to begin softening my soul with great swaths of grace and mighty depths of love. As I read my Bible, it became alive in its words to me, directed straight as an arrow to my heart, calling me always higher and higher, filling me with great peace.

I found God during these years of great want and sorrow. He filled my home—every inch, every dark corner—with the light of his love. And even though I was deserted with four babies, poor and alone, I look back at those years as being some of the most beautiful of my entire life. We were wrapped in the arms of a loving Heavenly Father who saved us. And despite our poverty and abandonment, we were rich with the overflowing care and love of God.

WHO AM I TO GOD?

I am, first and foremost, a daughter of the most benevolent, mighty, and loving heavenly Father. In the complexities, traumas, and hardships of my childhood, adolescence, and young adulthood, he stood firm by my side. After I was converted to Christianity, I recognized I had some healing to go through, but I wasn't sure how to talk about this yet, or even how to pray about it. That came years later.

Many years after I divorced, I moved to Michigan to complete my Ph.D. in counseling psychology. As a doctoral student, I worked anywhere from 15-17-hour days without a break. My alarm would go off at 3:40 a.m. every single weekday as I had to be at work by 5 a.m. I would often cry when I heard that alarm, and I'd whisper to God, "I can't go again." The faces of my children would come to mind, and I felt strengthened to get up yet again. Since that time, my waking prayer has been, "Give me the strength, energy, and cheerfulness for my day."

One evening, after a particularly difficult day, depleted of all hope and will, I knelt down by my bed and sobbed. The years' memories came to choke me. I began from my childhood, asking God, "Do you remember that?" and "Were you there when…?" and "Did you know this happened to me?" I traveled through my life and in one experience after another, the Lord validated every single painful thing I had lived through. When I rose from my knees, I felt such peace that I cannot explain, and I was assured, "Yes, Sarah, I was right there with you." I felt the warmth of his love and compassion toward me in a deeper way than ever before. This forever changed my prayer life. I opened up as never before and just talked to God as I would to a friend.

TODAY

So who am I today? Now that my children are grown and so many years have traveled by, I am still the mother of those four children who are the best parts of my life! Those years of raising them and being called to faithfulness, self-care, health, wholeness, and contentment as a woman, by necessity developed talents in me I didn't know I had.

My first discovered talent that began to blossom started in the kitchen. The kitchen became the center of our home, the sanctuary of my work as a mother. It was there I learned to cook, to trust my intuition, to follow directions only to learn the skills and to break free to develop my own dishes. Bounties from the earth, potatoes, whole wheat flour, rice milk, olive oil, sea salt, romaine lettuce, heirloom tomatoes, Cuban black beans, eggplant and shallots, oats and wild Minnesota rice, cherries, and minestrone soups, fed the bellies and souls of my children, keeping their eyes bright and sparkly, and their bodies thriving and blossoming. Food and its preparation were taught to me through poverty when my cupboards were bare, but if I had a little flour, a little oil, and some vegetables, I found ways to make wonderful meals.

I've also discovered a passion for bread. Making sourdough bread, with the influences of water and air temperatures, the freshness of the flour, and humidity levels, all combine to create rustic loaves of bread that are reminiscent of days reflected in art museums; of men sitting at a large block table after a day's hard work in the fields, tearing hunks of sourdough bread off a loaf and dipping it in olive oil before eating. Food is deeply religious, psychological, emotional, and an essential necessity of life. We are given the earth to glean our foods, with unlimited varieties and combinations.

I am now the wife of a man who has shown me the face of God; who has been my source of healing, hope, love, acceptance, and perfect freedom. He is my most extravagant gift from God. Our lives together are lived well, as he patiently and continually provides for my comfort and health. He sees me. He hears me. He knows my greatest strengths and my hardest falls. He quietly listens to me when I cry, offering a kiss on my hand and the reassurance that everything will be ok. He is faithful to our marriage and to his calling from God. He diligently cares for our relationship, nurturing us with thoughtful words, actions, and intentionality in all he does. We pray together every day, and in his prayers for me, I am aware of how deeply he knows God's heart of love and goodness. My husband calls on God like he is his friend.

I have finally met all requirements to graduate in August. I began school when my youngest daughter started second grade, and my years of undergraduate and graduate school and now completing this last year of my Ph.D. have been brutal! While in school full-time, I was managing a household, working at the church school to help pay for my children's tuition, semester after semester, year after year, working with all my might to excel in all the realms of life that were mine to manage. But I felt called to my field. I felt called to be a light to those in the dark and to give hope and healing to as many as possible. I love my work as a psychologist. And all the grueling years I had to trudge through to get here—to the end of my academic journey— only made me stronger.

I come from a family of creatives. My dad was an abstract painter, my sister is a portrait artist, my mom completed many fiber works when I was a child, and both of my grandparents were craftspeople. I love the canvas. I love the paint. There are moments with each work when I need to step back and "listen" to what the canvas is telling me; I have learned not to be in a rush or to be controlling or nervous while painting or all these pressures and stressors show through my brush strokes and colors. While painting, I am transported to a space where my heart and emotions bypass my higher-order, analytical thinking and I transfer my anguish, anger, shame and sadness, joy and exuberance right onto the canvas.

Most of my paintings have several "failed" paintings underneath. The more layers there are of "failed" paintings, the richer and more textured the final piece. In this, I have learned there are no mistakes. A new story is painted over and we become fuller in character and more complex in our beauty. As artists, we are allowed to share and partake in God's creativity.

The outdoors are a wide open space in which we are meant to explore, heal, decompress, vent, and expend our energy, trading our stress for renewal and rest. Hiking and running have brought me through many seasons of life. The miles I've traveled by foot have allowed for the heaviness in my soul to be tossed by the road/trailside. The wide-open skies of Colorado, the mountain vistas, the great Lake Michigan beaches, miles and miles through wooded paths that wind on their way. All have been places where I am aware there is a greater power than me, and I am humbled always. My frets and worries dissipate as the breezes dance with the trees, the waves of the lake splash at my feet, and the clouds form across the sky according to the wind which touches them. Sunsets and sunrises, storms that roll in and threaten, and seasons as they come and go, all speak to me of the heart of God. The sky overhead is his canvas; some days are wild, some are calm, but in them all, I recognize that God has his depths too, and he understands mine.

HOW I WORSHIP

I go to God the moment I wake up, early mornings before the rush of the world begins, where I hear Him through His word and I know that I am known. The depths of my soul, so often complicated and stormy to me, are met with the depth of God's soul. I am renewed every morning and were it not for the grace of God during these times of my life, in my daily communing with Him, I would not have survived many seasons. He meets me just as I am. He already knows the darkness that abounds in me before I realize those depths myself. He created me as an Artist who creates a painting, with layers of color and broken lines, the darkness of dark in the shadows, and the brightness of light in the illumination. He loves authenticity. It's we who seek to conform and mold ourselves after standards that are ordained by the world and not by God. I believe He loves my complex thoughts and emotions. When I look across the lake where my husband and I live, and I see a dark storm rolling across the sky, causing the leaves and branches of the trees to bend and blow in the wind, a thrill of energy and excitement fills my soul. My favorite weather pattern is the power and beauty of a storm when the blue sky is overcome with black clouds. In the same way, I believe God meets me during our time in the morning. He sometimes sees my heart reeling in a storm, and an energizing smile spreads across his face as he meets me. "Good morning, Sarah. Let's enter this storm together."

I intentionally meet with God, just as I am. When I was younger, I was so afraid of displeasing God as I met with him. I would have thoughts like, "Perhaps I should have sat down with my Bible earlier," or "Maybe I am too full of emotions and I will annoy him," or "Maybe I've displeased him in some way and he won't meet with me here." I'd fear his abandonment and fit myself up to be "perfect" so I could win his attention.

But it was in the very messiness of my life, where I never imagined God wanted to go, where I imagined he would run away—this was the very place where I experienced God running toward me.

We can get so caught up in being accepted through our performances and attempted "perfections." We can become so legalistic that we completely overlook God's desire for us. His greatest pleasure and joy are in spending time with us. He knows how different and varying each of our individual stories is; he knows how we are all wired differently, and he meets us where we are, just as we are, knowing us better than we know ourselves.

We hide and shield, manipulate, and lie to "trick" God into only seeing our acceptable parts, but God illuminates the soul. Not only for us to know ourselves more fully and authentically as we are, but in the very act of looking toward us, God's gaze is illuminating. We don't need to hide; he knows it all. And he still wants to meet with us—not to scold or correct or display power or anger—but simply to abide with us, comforting, guiding, leading, soothing, strengthening, and binding our hearts closer to his own.

Each of my children has different ways in which they would bid for my attention and affection. As a baby, Anna would continually cry for me to hold her. Even as a teenager, through her angsty and rebellious phase, she would climb on my lap or sit close to me, tucked into my side. In contrast, her sister, Marie, had a continual "don't touch" posture toward me. Even as a baby, she wasn't affectionate, and as a toddler she'd cry if I had to hold her hand, pulling it away as hard as she could. But Marie is also the child who will pull me into conversations about the deep matters of life. She has an enormous capacity for staying in nuanced spaces where there are no answers, but where she wants to talk of the things of God and the soul, and loss, and of trying to find her way. Anna spoke little of these things with me but pulled me physically by her side to find her comfort and safety.

Could you imagine if I ever told Marie, "I'm sorry, but you don't want to hold my hand, so I don't want to be with you today"? Or if I shared with Anna, "Unless you talk more and tell me what's going on, I don't want you near me"? Besides it being heartbreaking for any child to hear this from a parent, this could never come from the loving heart of a mother. My heart thrills that my children desire to spend time with me. I adapt to what they need. I listen to how they talk. I feel how they feel.

My greatest, most lofty, and most powerful feelings of love that I have for my children pale in comparison to God's love for us. I am sinful with storms. But God is never changing, without shadow or turning, and He is the embodiment of love itself. However we come to Him, whether stormy, quiet, questioning, doubting, angry, tired, angsty, confused, with feelings of rebelliousness or surrender, it matters not to Him. He adapts Himself to our personality type, moods, circumstances, and the makeup of our minds and hearts. He meets us fully just as we are.

My mind is very active and awake early in the morning. My devotional time is full of energy and praise, sometimes tears and sorrow, sometimes complaint and frustration. I journal and read and pray and am alive in God's presence. My husband, on the other hand, is not a morning person. I would never try to engage him in a deep conversation early in the morning; it would be a solo conversation with myself. He doesn't meet the Lord with a flurry of thoughts and words and emotions like I do. He is still and quiet. He contemplates and steadily and slowly allows his mind to wake up in God's presence. Some days, he walks or sits in his Amish rocker to pray above the water. We are very different in how we approach God, just like my children are very different in how they approach me.

God's heart rushes with joy simply to be invited by our side. He is our greatest Friend and our truest and most tender Father, and we are his children. I encourage you to meet with God, just as you are, who you are, where you are, and how you are. Bring to him your story. He's been closer than your very breath your entire life; he knows it all, and yet wants to talk with you about the details, the trauma, the sorrows, the joys, the mountain peaks, and the low valleys. He made you and fashioned you to be unique, one-of-a-kind, and no other like you. Trust that you will be met with acceptance by our Maker who calls you with a smile and a ravishing heart to fill you and make your life burn for greater things than this world could ever give.

If God can accept and save me, then I have pure and unquenching faith that he can accept anyone! He has pulled me out of more pits than I can count. I have challenged him, and I am sure there were many times he looked over at me and sighed, "Oh child, just come to me before you make a bigger mess." I simply meet with the Lord, every single day, just as I am, whether I feel a mess or am feeling pretty put together that morning. Neither matters. He loves me just the same. And he loves you, just the same.

Part 3
Real World Application and Examples

Now, this is where the fun begins! How do we live out and practice the things we are talking about in parts 1 & 2? If we don't get to real world application, we have just another great model/theory/theology/philosophy. This is one of the great problems with Christianity—we often fail to practice what we preach because the lessons never get from our heads into our hearts and out to the world through our hands and voices. This is why I wanted to talk about devotional life before talking about implementation. Devotional life is where the discipleship model and theology moves from our heads into our hearts as we spend time with Jesus. Now it's time to look at how our hearts can overflow into the lives of children through our hands and voices.

The following chapters are put together based on my experiences in 26 years of ministry to youth and young adults where I started out running student colporteur programs for six years and then ran campus-based youth ministries for 20 years at both denominational and public schools. This is where the rubber meets the road. My driving passion the whole time was to help young people live their faith by showing up on their turf—at school—where I could help them apply faith to life in the real world where they lived. This is the heart and soul of true Christian community.

In my church school ministry class at the seminary, I have my students create Church School Discipleship Plans which involve these specific discipling activities applied to their individual demographics and contexts. It's important to keep in mind that my students are from around the world. This means that although the outline and guiding principles are the same, individual practices and applications will vary widely in order to be culturally relevant and meaningful.

Here are the 6 discipling activities I use in my discipleship process:

1. Bonding: developing a relationship with the student

2. Devotional teaching: nurturing student's relationship with Jesus

3. Doctrinal teaching: showing students Jesus' truth and how all of scripture relates to him

4. Outreach: teaching students to see the world with fresh eyes and see the needs of others

5. Evangelism: seeking to make friendships with others so you can connect them to Jesus

6. Worship: Praising Jesus as he walks with you through the process

I'm sure there are other elements which could be added to my list, but these will at least help us get started and understand the progression that needs to take place to truly disciple young people.

One of the biggest weaknesses I've seen in discipling young people is the tendency to include only bonding and doctrinal teaching, and sometimes only one or the other. But if we want to truly make disciples, we must be very intentional about including the entire range of activities, and the progression which involves all the elements included in the list. In my experience, all are necessary; none are optional.

Chapter 9

Elementary (K-8) Church School Discipleship Action Plan

Frequently church strategic plans will start in August when families come back after summers of busyness and settle back into church life and school routine. But as a full-time youth pastor I typically began my church school campus ministries calendar in May/June. The reason for this is mostly because this is when the 8th graders from my elementary school graduated and transitioned into the youth group and activities. This gave me the summer months for bonding those youth into the group. Many of them I already knew from the elementary years, but there were also those coming from nearby elementary schools with whom I hadn't yet become acquainted. Additionally, in my church Vacation Bible School, during which I served as leader for the games, was typically toward the beginning of summer—sometime around mid-June. This was pure bonding time with all the kids from my church—from tiny tots up into the middle of elementary school. We had lots of fun playing tag, duck-duck-goose, and other simple childhood games.

This was also a time for challenging the older elementary and academy students to serve in leadership roles. From small group leaders, to helping in the kitchen, to being my games assistant, there was a variety of roles to be filled which mostly involved bonding throughout the VBS sessions. I was also able to share devotional thoughts with the student leaders each morning to inspire them to serve well and from their hearts. VBS was my first bookend with the elementary-aged kids during the summer, and the other bookend was graduation and them joining youth group. (We will talk more about this in the next section on academy discipleship.)

Other than VBS and passing through the children's Sabbath School divisions from time to time, my summers were primarily focused on youth activities. My other elementary school activities revolved around being on campus once school started in August.

Here is a list of my main activities followed by descriptions and goals. They are listed according to the categories above for reference. Without clear goals for each activity, I may not have had as clear of a sense of purpose as I could have, but having achievable goals helped me be intentional and more effective at making sure my goals were met.

Bonding

CURBSIDE VISITATION

A great way to engage in visitation with both parents and children is to be outside on the sidewalk when kids are dropped off in the morning, and when they are being picked up in the afternoon. It gives you a great opportunity for hellos, high fives, or fist bumps. Parents and grandparents appreciate seeing you there with their kids and invested in the church school. Kids also love seeing that you care enough to show up, even though they may not be able to verbalize it, but you can certainly tell by the smile on their faces when they see you.

When I was a seminary student some years ago, my youth ministry professor shared the concept of visitation with young people. In my experience, when I went to visit them at home, I was really seeing the parents. Though the kids were there at home, it was never anything like when I visited them at school. At school, I see their friends, their environment, and the support systems and challenges they have daily. At school, the teachers also let me know of any difficult circumstances they know the kids and their families may be facing at home. Teachers tend to know a lot about what is going on in the lives of their students because they spend so much time together. and partnering with them can give me a heads up so I can be of support to families experiencing difficulties.

PLAYING AT RECESS

Playing with the kids at recess is also great bonding time. Of course, it is much simpler to build relationships with younger children than it is with older kids and adults. It is relatively common to receive lots of hugs from kids you may not even know yet, simply by walking into a kindergarten classroom. At this age, kids tend to love and trust adults and a simple wave or high five can be all it takes to have a new friend. Five minutes a day passing through the lower grades during lunchtime is a great start at being visible to the kids, and the initiation of relationships which will continue to grow as they develop over the years.

Devotional Teaching
T.A.G. (TIME ALONE WITH GOD)

TAG is one of the greatest and most inspiring activities I have ever witnessed! The first time I saw it was in a 3rd grade classroom in the Oregon Conference. The teacher gave the children a block of time to spend in personal devotions. They could listen to Christian music, read their Bibles, color in a Bible coloring book, draw, journal, or spend time encountering God in whatever way they wanted. The teacher had soft instrumental music playing in the background and was encouraging, directing individual students one at a time through a whisper.

I didn't talk to the teacher about this, but I would imagine her own personal devotional time with Jesus and her own passion for her relationship with him was the driving force behind this activity. I've heard other teachers talk about TAG as well—but this is where I personally witnessed it for the first time, and it was absolutely breathtaking to watch little 3rd grade children deeply engrossed in personal devotions.

One of my seminary students who witnessed TAG in the same classroom a year earlier quoted one little girl who said, "Without TAG, my life would fall apart." This is the foundation of well-established discipleship!

LUNCHTIME SMALL GROUPS

Through my experience running Christian clubs in Adventist elementary junior high, academies, and public high schools, I learned lunchtime is not a good time for Bible study. In the middle of a day full of academic studying, the last thing students want during lunch is to study more.

So my lunchtime groups always focused on discipling students with fellowship and devotional time.

Devotional time is much different than study time, as we saw in the last section of this book. These lunchtime groups are where I would begin laying the foundation for helping young people find their own relationship with Jesus and learn how to nurture it. We would begin with a check-in time and take prayer requests as a way of building community—discipleship cannot happen well without community. Sometimes the discipling community may be just disciple and discipler, but making room for more is always good.

For the devotional we would discuss something from my devotions that day or perhaps from something one of the young people experienced in theirs. We would discuss how to be better friends with Jesus, how to pray throughout the day in any situation, something along a devotional theme, or something one of their friends was struggling with. (Hopefully all the devotional ideas in the last section opened your mind to things that nurture individuals devotionally which you can share as well.)

A NOTE ON ENCOUNTER BIBLE CURRICULUM

We will talk more about the Encounter curriculum in the academy chapter, but I want to note here that this new Bible curriculum is life-changing for both students and teachers of grades K-12. In the world divisions where this curriculum is being used, the testimonies of lives changed are powerful! You can visit encounter.adventisteducation.org to get an overview. Teachers are all familiar with this, and pastors would do well to take some time to study these tools. Encounter is a combination of both devotional teaching and deep study; the Bible is the textbook, and the focus is on leading kids into a personal relationship with Jesus—it's powerful stuff!

Doctrinal Teaching
BAPTISM CLASSES

Just because lunchtime is not always a good time for Bible study doesn't mean we can't study with kids on campus—it just means we need to find a better time. I always found it easy to partner with the teachers to teach baptism classes during Bible class time in the mornings.

At one school where I was youth pastor, the teachers always made Bible class the first class of the day. The principal worked together with the teachers to coordinate me taking interested kids for baptism study time during Bible class. They agreed that students in my baptismal class did not have to make up the classroom Bible lesson for the day. This made it fun and exciting for the kids to get to go with me to the library and study the distinctive doctrinal truths of our denomination. The kids would still, obviously, be exposed to the rest of the Bible class lesson they were missing in the classroom—they just didn't have to make up the homework. Instead, they filled in the baptism books I would provide as we studied through the topics.

This was a great way for me to begin bonding with elementary kids beyond VBS games and simple greetings while walking around campus. A typical schedule was pre-baptism class for 5th grade on Monday mornings, then baptism classes for 6th grade on Tuesday mornings, 7th grade on Wednesday mornings, and 8th grade on Thursday mornings. Students were always welcomed back year after year even if they had already been baptized.

I'm so grateful to all the elementary school teachers who gave me this great opportunity to spend time with kids at school year after year—this formed the foundation and beginnings of my relationship building and discipling of the younger children. For me, this age is such a fun time to be with kids who are generally happy, eager, and engaged learners. I have lots of great memories from these classes!

Outreach

COMMUNITY SERVICE DAYS AND MORE

Community service is lifestyle evangelism and an important step in helping our kids find and exercise their faith. In their journey to faith, sometimes young people can have a hard time relating to teachings about God as a first step, and their faith journey may begin with outreach. Sometimes the spark for a relationship with Jesus comes through helping those in need or simply helping make your community a better place.

At one school where I worked, I was a part of a committee evaluating the WASC (Western Association of Schools and Colleges) report. The school had been told they needed to build a better community service program. At the time, first grade was regularly passing out little loaves of banana bread to the homes in the community around the school, 2nd through 4th grades each had their own projects (I just can't remember what they were) as well, and 5th grade was regularly going to sing and serve at local nursing homes. The problem was with the junior high classrooms, so I helped the school as they formed a plan.

I suggested and helped to build a junior high community service model was based on the existing academy model, since at this particular school, junior high students moved from classroom to classroom like in high school, making scheduling community service a bit more challenging than simply choosing a classroom project. I suggested creating a Friday community service day in which all junior high students could engage together, rather than by grade.

So, once per quarter, community service day started with an assembly during which a parent or other community member would talk about why they believed community service was important. For example, one parent talked about why they were a member of Kiwanis, and another time I had the director of the local city parks and recreation department talk about why they loved to have volunteers clean up parks and help plant trees, etc.

Other community service projects included Adopt-a-Highway cleanup, feeding the homeless, volunteering at the local food bank or the Ronald McDonald House, cleaning up a future park site, and more. Those who forgot to get their permission slip signed to go off-campus would stay at school and clean up around the grounds, help the maintenance manager with odd jobs, or help teachers in the lower grades with projects.

At the end of the day, we all gathered together in the chapel to share stories from the day, which many times involved miraculous interactions. It's always important to share the stories from the day so any kids who may have had a boring or even perhaps a bad day, could hear something inspiring to encourage them that they could have a better experience next time.

There are so many ways to engage with the community, and we can't cover them all here, but let me just list a few more that can be hosted on your school campus and to which you can invite the community. I'm not going to describe them all here, but maybe these titles can get your imagination started: Pet and Hobby Fair, Apple Festival, Christmas Program, 5k Charity Run (to benefit a local non-profit). Additionally, community-oriented events which typically happen at churches can often get a better turnout when hosted at a school because the general public tends to be more open to going to a school than to a church. For more on this see my collaborativeministry.org website and click on the "community care and involvement" tab after watching the intro video.

Evangelism

STUDENT-LED EVANGELISTIC SERIES

This is an example of the equipping phase of discipleship, and the primary example I learned from children and family discipleship pastor Ben Martin. Pastor Ben created an event called "The Tent." This is a local evangelistic series which takes place in a meeting tent pitched behind the Alumni House on the campus of Andrews University. Pastor Ben and the faculty and staff at Ruth Murdoch Elementary School (on the campus of Andrews University) spend the whole school year helping junior students write and practice delivering sermons for the series. The students are also taught how to do absolutely everything in this series of meeting. They serve as greeters, run the PA and lighting systems, set up the chairs, etc. It is 100 percent student-run, every student is involved, and each is assisted in finding their gifts and where they fit best into the team. I find this to be a brilliant way to help kids be equipped for service as disciples of Jesus. And every year, there are baptisms as a result of the meetings. In particular, the year previous to my writing this book a great revival broke out with many requests for Bible studies and baptisms!

Pastor Ben also has 7th- and 8th-graders write Bible study lessons they use to teach baptism classes for younger children. I won't go into detail here, but Pastor Ben will have a small group of junior high kids each choose a doctrinal topic to write a lesson on, and then they all go together to a lower grade classroom and take turns teaching each week while the other students in the group go desk-to-desk helping the participants look up the texts and answer the questions. This is a fantastic way to help those 7th- and 8th- graders really understand, own, and share their faith.

Worship

CLASSROOM WORSHIPS AND WEEK OF PRAYER SPEAKERS

Classroom worships and weeks of prayer are opportunities for pastors and other adults to share their testimony of faith in Jesus through heartfelt talks, testimonies, and stories to give young people a chance to see what faith in action looks like. Worships and chapels also offer opportunities to sing and worship together. Worshiping together with their peers at school will help young people feel more familiar with the worship services at church. In turn, hopefully school worships will have an impact on how worship services at church are conducted, as pastors learn to make church worship more relevant to felt and known needs of the church's young people.

Daily worship during a week of prayer is also a great way to build relationships with the students which will help them respond positively to a call to join on-campus baptism classes after the week of prayer is over. This is how worship can lead into doctrinal and devotional study (I always included both in my baptism classes), and help build authentic Christian community.

The other example I would like to refer to here is in relation to the Three-Story concept as discussed in chapter 4. Three-Story can be a great way to help kids discover their own personal testimony and share it as a worship talk in various classrooms with younger children. It can also be used for sermons in church when you have 2-3 young people whose Three-Stories all go together and can be shared back-to-back.

These are just some of the activities I engaged in personally or have heard about that can be utilized with elementary church school students. I hope this gives you some good ideas of what you can do and inspires you to be creative and engage in ways that are unique to you and the community where you live.

In the Valuegenesis research surveys, Academy students claimed that some of the most important factors in forming their faith were attending church school, Bible class, school weeks of prayer, student-led weeks of prayer, and their Bible teacher.[1] There are other studies which show pastoral involvement in church school has a very important positive impact on young people's spirituality as well.[2] As we close this chapter, I'd like to share the testimony of one of my students who is now a youth director and how she ministered to elementary school students on campus when she was young.

---

[1] John Wesley Taylor, "Joining and Remaining," Journal of Adventist Education, April/June 2017

[2] https://www.ministrymagazine.org/archive/2017/06/The-pastor-and-the-church-school

PING

I am the only Seventh-day Adventist or Christian in my family. Most of my family members are atheist, while some are polytheists. On the other hand, I became Christian after three years of Bible study with the school chaplain in Tai Po Sam Yuk secondary school, and I am going to share how my middle school and high school worked together to reach students in the elementary school.

My middle school, high school, and church cooperated with each other to hold a program called EQ for the elementary school students. They wanted to approach the residents who lived around the campus and church and introduce the middle and high school to the public, share the gospel with them, and, at the same time, provide the church and school pastors an opportunity to connect with both the locals and the parents of the students.

I started to use what I had learned from the Bible in the leadership training program the church and school put on, and the school chaplain invited me as a student helper to take care of the kids and get them involved in all the events of the program. I helped with worship song-leading, Bible story-telling, games, cooking, and reading for the programs we put on for the elementary grades. Through filling this role, I learned to be patient, brave, caring, and firm.

As I learned and experienced a lot of grace and power from God, I started to share my own testimony with others. I was invited to share my testimony at vespers, and I felt more comfortable and excited to share my story in front of people. I used to be the one to sit and listen to the testimonies from others, but after the discipleship experience, I became the one sharing on stage and encouraging people to keep and strengthen their faith in God.

When I was a student, I did not realize that the church pastors and school chaplains were giving me discipleship. I now realize they spent a lot of time and provided a lot of materials and needs for me to build up my relationship with God and strengthen my faith in him.

Activity for This Chapter

Create a list of the activities you can do with elementary age kids, and reach out to your local elementary/middle school. Ask if there are any ways you can volunteer at the school, and start becoming a present support for the students.

# Chapter 10

Academy (9-12) Discipleship Action Plan

Just as the formative elementary years are crucial in molding and shaping the student's life and spiritual walk with God, the high school years are vital as well. During these years, students tend to struggle with their identity, relationships, and purpose in life. Developmentally, high school students are capable of deeper relationships than early elementary students, and junior high students are developing somewhere in between. Along with the ability for deeper relationships, the need for more adult discipling is very real as well.[1]

Before we get into specific discipling activities to use to engage with high school students, I want to begin with some stories a few of my students have shared which include their own struggles and progress through their high school years. They share not only their high school journeys, but also the impact of important disciplers they had.

CHRISTELLE

My story isn't too complex. I grew up as a pastor's kid, since my dad was a pastor for the Adventist church, and that inadvertently came with a lot of pressure and expectations. However, I didn't mind

---

[1] For more information on teenage developmental issues, refer to Appendix B.

having all of that responsibility; I grew up believing I was perfect and that I was better than everyone else because of who I was and who my father was. Yet as I began to grow older, I realized I was still dissatisfied with a few things in life. I believe that's why I turned to TV and entertainment to give me the escape I wanted. I thought my life was too boring, being such a goody two shoes, but I didn't really want the perception of who I had crafted to be to be broken. So that was why I turned to those idols.

When senior year of high school came about I really wanted to start taking my walk with God seriously. I started being more receptive to my teachers' testimonies, and to certain pastors who would come and talk about their experiences with God. During a trip senior year, I finally understood that God truly does love me and what that meant to me. I fell in love with God that day and truly began my journey as a Christian.

That same year, my English teacher had us start reading "The Great Controversy" by Ellen White, and that is where my relationship with God began to really deepen and take off. Not only was I excited to be learning more about God through White's writings, but I was also seeing Christ being lived out through my English teacher.

I guess, at the end of the day, I was discipled early-on by my English teacher during my senior year of high school. She not only pointed us to Christ in what she taught us, but in how she acted and lived her life. She was a true maker of disciples through and through.

CARLOS

I want to emphasize the value of Adventist teachers in my discipleship journey. They were the ones who helped me to know Jesus more profoundly and gave me a role model to follow.

My religion teacher was the first person who discipled me as a child; I loved the way he presented Jesus to us through Scripture. He talked with me about Jesus' life, how he used to act when he was a young child, and how he treated others around him. I learned from my teacher his passion for talking about Jesus and keeping him in all his conversations. Since that year, I remember trying to apply his example when interacting with my friends and church members.

The other person who discipled me was another teacher, who became my friend. He taught us history and religion in high school, and he was a person who took Christianity seriously. He had an excellent way of teaching Bible principles and doctrines, and we learned to create an Adventist identity and embrace our mission in this world as a church. Also, he significantly impacted my life when I was a teenager. At that time, I made some mistakes that discouraged me so much, to the point of desisting from going to the seminary. He was there to listen and advise me to return to God and my calling.

HANNAH

Discipleship is a process of transformation. I have experienced this discipleship model in my own spiritual walk/growth with the Lord during high school. This discipleship led me to accept Jesus as my personal Savior, and in turn I was able to share Christ with my best friend.

My discipleship process really began developing in high school. I found myself searching for identity, belonging, and value; a relationship to help me navigate life. I had always felt a longing for this type of relationship but had tried filling it with romantic relationships or friendships. I had never really had a mentor to guide me in how to develop a walk with Christ. I would listen to my chaplain (fondly known as Chappy) share her experience with Christ during our high school chapels, and her testimony piqued my interest. Eventually I was able to work for her as a student worker and was able to see firsthand what her relationship with Christ truly looked like "offstage." Chappy's relationship represented the relational aspect I was craving as a teen. Thus, I truly began committing myself to daily devotionals and mission trips.

Through these personal devotionals, I began to understand the beauty of a relationship with Christ. I started realizing how much I enjoyed developing this, and in turn wanted to share it. As mission trips became a lifestyle, I also started finding areas in church ministry of which I could be a part. I desperately wanted to be involved in service.

Soon, I was helping in children and youth ministries at my local church, and I began truly displaying my walk with the Lord. Throughout this transformation, one of my best friends chose to give Jesus a genuinely committed try too, and eventually she was baptized.

That was an exciting day for me to witness! Now I hope to keep discipling.

These testimonies from my seminary students are such an inspiring gift! They are a true testimony of the powerful influence of Adventist educators, pastors, and parents. It's nice to be reminded we are getting many things right!

My youth ministry style is really a product of my personality. I am an introvert by nature, and it takes me some time to build relationships. I was never the stereotypical life of the party; the guitar-playing fun youth pastor (and yet, within my own style, I could have fun with kids). I found my best years were when I was between the ages of 40-50 years old—when I was more like a father figure as the youth pastor.

Because of my relational nature rather than entertaining nature, I found that a long-term tenure worked best with my style, so I was at my last church for 14 years. I dug in with relationships in the elementary years as described in the last chapter, and then kept a daily presence on campus at the academy, volunteering as the art teacher every day, and other roles I'll describe below. I also ran lots of trips because that was where I could especially take the relationships deeper.

I have found that when I'm on the road with kids—camping, eating, working, and doing ministry together—a great bond has time to form. I'd take kids on trips to places they had never been and would never have the opportunity to go to if it wasn't for this school trip Many kids really needed the time away from home and the drama that can sometimes come with teenagers in the house. I seemed to be that other father figure kids could open up to when they felt misunderstood or judged at home. And even if a teen's home life was good, it's always great to have an extra "dad" around. I also always had great female sponsors on my trips who were the well-accepted mother figures on campus or from church. Everyone needs at least a couple of moms!

After my 14 years in Lodi, California, the graduating seniors who had lived in the area for at least that long couldn't remember a time when I wasn't part of their lives. We lived a lot of stories together—memorable stories we will never forget. Similar to Jesus' ministry, there was a smaller inner circle present with me for the most time in my ministry, a bigger circle which was just a little more distant but involved, and then the majority who came and went on the fringes. But all could see the stories we were living in daily life and on special trips, and could engage as closely or distantly as they chose.

With younger elementary school kids, relationships are built more quickly and easily as we talked about in the last chapter; they really don't require that much time. But in this chapter, you will notice that deeper relationships are key. If we keep on just scheduling activities, even if they are high quality and entertaining, they will ultimately fall short unless they lead to an opportunity for a relationship with you personally, or with another pastor, teacher, or adult volunteer. I always surrounded myself with as many volunteer leaders as I could because I knew I could not connect deeply with every student. The more volunteers I had on my team, the more opportunities there were for kids to connect with at least one caring, discipling adult open to a relationship with them. Valuegenesis shows this is one of the great strengths of Adventist education—the numbers of caring adults on campus with whom our young people have opportunity to connect.

My goal in youth ministry was to make sure all the students knew the opportunity for engagement was there. I wanted to live my faith out loud as a testimony for all to see and allow students to participate as they chose.

One of my volunteer leaders in Fresno, California, had worked directly with Jose Rojas when he was youth director in that area years before. She said he had told her that in youth ministry, don't expect to see anything happen. He told her she was planting seeds which would one day bear fruit she may not ever see. I have found this to be wise advice and still pass it on to my seminary students today.

Something to note is that we all have different levels at which we can give during the various phases of life and we need to keep a balance with family. When my kids were preschoolers, I didn't do Friday night vespers because that time was special for my family. Later, when my kids were teens, I started doing vespers on Friday nights. Some of us can have five very deep discipling relationships and dozens of kids on the fringes, while others may only be able to go deep with two or three, with and ten on the fringes. Always be sure to work in your own armor. This is one of the reasons it is important to understand your love languages, learning styles, devotional style, and how you connect in relationships best.

Below you'll find some of my major youth ministry activities, broken down and arranged in the order of Discipling Activities laid out in the last chapter: bonding, devotional study, doctrinal study, outreach, evangelism, and worship. I always scheduled my annual calendar starting with bonding because that logically needs to happen before students will come on outreach and mission trips.

Lake Shasta Houseboat Trip
DISCIPLING ACTIVITIES: BONDING, DEVOTIONAL STUDY, AND WORSHIP

Description: When I moved to Lodi, I inherited a trip which had been happening for many years and was well-loved by students and many parents. It was a fun trip, and I was expected to keep the tradition going, so I did, setting specific goals for the trip so it would fit within my specific discipleship plan.

As a trip designed to give kids a fun break the week after high school graduation, it was a perfect opportunity to get to know them. The trip was Monday through Friday on a lake in the mountains three hours away. Two adult sponsors came to cook, and four or five sponsors also brought their boats so the kids could spend all day on the water learning or perfecting the watersport of their choice. Total, we had around six to eight adults and 30-50 kids. Students were eligible to participate as incoming first year high schoolers through to just-graduated seniors. There was a fee, but I never let finances stop any student from coming. I would sponsor fundraisers and find donors to make sure no one who wanted to go was left behind.

We had fun all day long as we taught kids to wakeboard or wake surf, with certain sponsors assigned to make sure the kids were safe as they had fun. My cooks were the best, and the kids loved the food. They could eat all they wanted pretty much any time of day, and with this joyful atmosphere, it was easy to bond and make new friends. This is where I got to know a large number of kids, both when I was new, and when some of them were.

The best part of the trip was in the evenings after everyone was tired from playing all day. We would have worship together on top of the houseboats at sunset and the theme was always on devotional life and relationship with Jesus. Our secondary focus was on nature and the opportunities they had to spend time with Jesus outdoors while we were there in the middle of the mountains on a beautiful lake. After worship, there was dessert and social time before bed.

At bedtime, the only option for staying up late was to be in a small group conversation with me. Those conversations would go late into the night, and this is the time and place where kids really opened up freely about their doubts about God or questions about why they weren't supposed to do this or that. The rule was "any topic goes," and any question could be asked as long as it was done respectfully. When kids are away from home on a trip and exhausted late at night, they get very open and honest. These are some of the best discussions I've ever had as a youth pastor.

Senior Yosemite Trip
DISCIPLING ACTIVITIES: BONDING, DEVOTIONAL STUDY AND WORSHIP

Description: This is a school-sponsored trip I was invited to join. This means it was an easy trip with no planning on my part, so I am only reporting on the activities I led, rather than on the whole trip.

As a full-time youth pastor, I had the privilege of being 100 percent youth-focused all the time. Most youth pastors have other responsibilities as well, so I was in a unique position which allowed me to do a lot, especially after 14 years in one place. If you are not a full-time youth pastor, trips like this one planned by others are great! All you have to do is take care of a few activities and spend the rest of the time bonding with kids and the other adult sponsors. You can even show up a little late and take off a little early if you need to.

This was a Wednesday through Sunday camping trip to Yosemite National Park, which was only a few hours away from the academy. Since the trip was school-run, I just showed up late Wednesday night to pitch my own tent—usually after everyone else was already sleeping. I was responsible for a team-building activity on Thursday morning, so I just had to show up for that on time and then stay for the Friday hike up Half Dome.

The team-building activity I created was focused on challenging the students in the senior class to create imaginary companies they may one day run, and recruit classmates for different roles in the company. This meant identifying and affirming talents they saw in each other. Next, I had them think of ways their companies could give back to society once they had become successful. So if students had formed a medical practice together, they would often decide to go on medical mission trips to help others for free, etc. The third challenge was to think of ways they could use their identified talents to make a positive impact on campus this year, now that they were seniors and were looked up to by the younger students. We always got some great implementable ideas!

My second responsibility was to bring up the rear on the Friday hike to the top of Half Dome. This is an approximately 17-mile hike up several thousand feet of rocky paths and granite steps chiseled out of the side of the mountains. For someone in reasonably good shape this is an 8-hour hike on average and a real test of grit. But there were times I was on the trail with struggling kids for 15 hours or more—one time I didn't get the last group down until nearly midnight. This was, of course, an exceptional situation in which a student had an asthma attack on top of Half Dome and we just had to take our time. Another time a girl's knees gave out and she couldn't go on. We were blessed to meet up with a forest ranger who was on his way down and was able to give her a piggy-back ride the rest of the way—he actually jogged down the trail for a couple hours with her on his back! I could go on for pages with incredible stories, but suffice to say, I've had the privilege of living some incredible stories with kids on this trip—stories we will never forget!

Art Class Teacher
DISCIPLING ACTIVITIES: BONDING

Description: As mentioned earlier, when I moved to Lodi I wanted to be on-campus with kids because I had learned after teaching Bible in Fresno that the opportunities on-campus for discipleship are great. When I asked if I could sit in on art class, the principal said, "There is no art class—why don't you start one?" Then a couple of years later a new principal came and made it a required class for first year students so I could have every student in a fun, non-threatening environment four days per week.

This is where I got to know kids well, and they got to know me too. After my art class became required, the opportunity for relationship-building meant that all my trips were filling up because of the relationships and reputation built in art class. Art class opened the doors to discipleship like nothing else did for me. Some youth pastors play basketball, some have shop night—I had art class.

I challenge you to think through your hobbies and interests and think of which ones you can bring to school to share with the students so you can get to know them, and they can get to know you. This is a great example of the beginning of the discipleship process.

Tuesday Chapels
DISCIPLING ACTIVITIES: DEVOTIONAL STUDY, WORSHIP

Description: Our academy had Chapel every day when I was working there, and Tuesday was the day I was in charge. A group of students decided they wanted to start a worship band, so I raised money for a sound system and some instruments. (I personally have no musical ability, so I left that to the kids! My job was to provide opportunity.)

This allowed for a better, more relevant worship experience, since it was student-led and gave the kids a chance to serve and lead. Then, as mentioned earlier, every week I worked with a student to create a Three-Story worship talk to share. Student-led bands and talks can go well and can also be a challenge, but through it all these were great opportunities to disciple kids very specifically in ways that can be a great spiritual experience for the entire campus. These were also some of the best opportunities I had to equip some of the students I was discipling to be leaders in ministry.

Wednesday Lunchtime Small Group

DISCIPLING ACTIVITIES: BONDING, DEVOTIONAL STUDY, DOCTRINAL STUDY AND OUTREACH

Description: One year on the senior Yosemite trip, at the end of the team-building activity (discussed above), when the students created lists of how they were going to lead spiritually on campus that year, one of the ideas shocked me. They asked me to start a Christian Club at the academy. They knew I ran Christian clubs at the local public high schools, and they asked me to do the same for them. I asked them why they wanted one—they already had Chapel and Bible class every day—and they said that Bible class was learning facts (before the Encounter curriculum)[2] and Chapel was a lecture from the principal. They knew my public high school clubs focused on Christian fellowship, devotional life, and outreach, and they wanted that too.

I was happy to have a small group meeting every week on Wednesdays at lunchtime. The principal went so far as to tell the staff that no other meetings could be held during that time so nothing would interfere with the kids who wanted to participate in my small group. We had an amazing group that year who attended faithfully and participated eagerly. I even had about a dozen kids from this experience who became one of the focus groups for my Doctor of Ministry research project on spiritual growth in the kids in my campus clubs.[3] I think the fact that it was part of my doctorate and contained focus groups, etc. inspired them as well as the content of what we did.

---

[2] For more information on this, refer to Appendix C.

[3] The full DMin Project Document can be found here: Ward, Scott R., "Faith Development Within the Campus-Based Youth Ministry Model of the English Oaks Adventist Church" (2014). Professional Dissertations DMin. 146. https://digitalcommons.andrews.edu/dmin/146

Outreach flowed from that group as our devotional lives grew. One of the results was that we decided to adopt the neighborhood around the school for monthly door-to-door outreach projects. By the end of the year, all the students claimed they had experienced significant spiritual growth because of their participation in the group.

In my research, I also had lunchtime small groups for grades 7-8 at our Adventist elementary school, as well as a group at the local High School. I've always felt this was the most successful year of my ministry because its structure made me more focused and consistent and I ended up writing what I taught in the groups in my book, "Authentic," which I mentioned earlier in this book. These are memories I will never forget, and the book which came from it continues to impact my seminary students today.

I ended up completely taking over the little chapel my small group met in and I opened it up every day during lunchtime for students who just wanted to drop in and chat or needed spiritual counseling, etc. It became the hub of my ministry presence at the academy.

Baptism Classes
DISCIPLING ACTIVITIES: BONDING, DEVOTIONAL STUDY AND DOCTRINAL STUDY

Description: I didn't have a lot of academy baptism classes, but from time-to-time there were some students who hadn't gotten baptized in elementary school and would tell me they were ready. We would then set up a time—usually with two to three students—and go through some doctrinal studies and a good overview of what it means to give your life to Jesus. This is when I also began to add teachings on devotional life to my baptism classes. My focus became one of making sure the students knew how to live out the teachings of the church. This focus was influenced by the success of my lunchtime groups, and I ended up including devotional life and relationship with Jesus to my elementary school baptism classes as well. This meant my baptism classes went for twice as long as a usual ten-week class, which helped me build even better relationships from which to disciple.

Youth With a Mission SF (YWAM)
DISCIPLING ACTIVITIES: BONDING, DEVOTIONAL STUDY, OUTREACH, EVANGELISM, AND WORSHIP

Description: Because of all the bonding and other discipling activities involved in the activities above, when it came time for outreach ministries, students knew and trusted me and wanted to go. Additionally, parents knew me and were willing to allow their kids to go. For this trip I partnered with the academy chaplain/Bible teacher—she signed kids up and found funding for those who needed it; I organized and ran the trip.

Youth with a Mission (YWAM) is a non-profit Christian organization with mission bases around the world which host teens and young adults who want to engage in ministry. The base in San Francisco is a houseless ministry facility in the Tenderloin District near downtown. Please note, if you ever want to do weekend houseless ministry trips, it is important to go with an existing organization which knows the area and can assure your safety. Since YWAM operates 365 days per year hosting group after group, they know the streets and many of the people living there.

At YWAM we were taught to engage in relational houseless ministry. In this type of ministry, the focus is on getting into conversation with people, which hopefully leads to sharing encouragement, prayer, and perhaps even a testimony. On Friday night after supper, we would have group orientation on how to be safe on the streets. We were taught things like always staying in groups with your leader and keeping your eyes open during prayer to be aware of your surroundings.

After orientation was hot chocolate ministry. For this we formed groups of three to four kids with an adult sponsor, each group taking a jug of hot chocolate and some cups. We went to the streets and offered hot chocolate to those seeking shelter there on the cold, misty San Francisco nights. This always led to conversations about how people are doing and requests for prayer. After an hour ministering with cocoa, we would come back for debrief and sharing.

On Sabbaths we took a similar approach for lunchtime. Everyone made two lunches—one for you, and one for the friend you were going to meet. We then went to the Civic Center area where lots of unhoused individuals spend their days, and when they saw us coming, they knew what was going on. We would sit in groups with the people we met and talk about life. The teens learned houseless people are valuable humans who have much to offer, rather than just seeing them as something "less."

In some conversations I heard homeless people begging the kids not to try drugs because just one time can make some people an addict. We were also able to share with the people we met that there were services at the YWAM base where they could shower, eat, join a 12-step program, and get job training. These times on the streets were some of the most impactful in my ministry. This trip became so popular that many years we went twice.

On Saturday nights we had a commitment service—a reflective time when students could think about their experiences on the streets and how it impacted their lives. There were stations for journaling, reading scripture, foot washing and communion, drawing, and more. There was soft Christian music in the background, and kids could lay on the carpeted floor to write and reflect, or sit on the couches. They could also talk to sponsors about what they were thinking or feeling if they chose to.

During this intensive reflective time of prayer, kids were often in tears and would need to talk, and mostly they wanted to talk to the academy chaplain/Bible teacher I partnered with on this trip. It might have been because she had become a mother-figure to them, spending time in scripture with them every day, or it may have been something else, but I was always very grateful for her partnership and the love she showed the students as we discipled them to Jesus.

There are obviously more activities like spring break mission trips, Friday night vespers, and others which are a standard part of youth ministry and academy life, but I think we have discussed enough to show the importance of building relationships with teens. Once again, this is my style based on who I am as a person. Lots of others engage in similar activities—just pick and choose which ones work for you, check out the dozens of other options out there in the youth ministry world, or make up your own ideas.

Personally, I found that on-campus activities and overnight trips are a great way to disciple kids for Jesus, and partnering with academy faculty and staff opens opportunities to be more effective together than we ever could be separately. Even if you are a senior pastor rather than a youth pastor, I hope you can identify here at least a couple of ways to get involved in discipling kids rather easily by partnering with your local church school.

Activity for This Chapter

Make a list of some of the activities in this chapter you resonated with and feel like you could make your own. Perhaps after reading through these activities new ones have come to mind, or you are remembering activities you experienced which resonated with you as a youth. Write them down and then see how you can get involved with these activities. Follow up with your local academy/high school, and see how you can start volunteering and being present with the students.

Chapter 11

Public School Discipleship Action Plan

Growing up I mostly attended church school, but I also experienced public school at every level. I attended public schools in 3rd, 9th and 10th grades, and after three years of Adventist college I spent three years at a public university and graduated there. So I understand first-hand the challenges of studying on a public campus. And from a pastoral perspective I have struggled with the fact that with public school students I did not have the same access to spending time with them and discipling them as I did with my kids in church school.

Another issue is that public schools don't operate and teach from the same Christian worldview our church schools do. At-risk behaviors are often greater at public schools, putting students at further disadvantage.

So what can we do when our young people don't have access to the benefits of church school ministry? We can't leave public school kids out—statistically they are most at risk of not staying in church.[1] For eight years I served as the NAD's first public high school ministries volunteer coordinator while also serving as a youth pastor. I can say from experience that we MUST do more! The church

---

[1] The Taylor article quoted earlier indicating the advantages and benefits of Adventist education also means that those not in Adventist education are not experiencing those advantages and benefits.

must do more, Adventist education must become more accessible, and public school parents need to be better supported because they have a much larger responsibility to carry when there is no church school to help disciple their children.

Currently, our best ministries to public elementary school children are Adventurers, Pathfinders, summer camp, and family ministries. Since many students either age out or drop out of these ministries after elementary school, focusing on ministries for high schoolers is critically important. In looking at K-12 public high school ministries beyond the existing ones mentioned above, I'm going to suggest two ministries which are more school-related where discipleship can happen. First is the concept of an elementary after-school program, and the second is public high school campus Christian clubs. But before we look at these two programs, I'd like you to hear from my seminary professor colleague, Abner Hernandez, as he shares his story about growing up in his country's public school system.

Christian Education at Home: My Experience

ABNER F. HERNANDEZ

I grew up in a Seventh-day Adventist family on the biggest island in the Caribbean Sea, Cuba, and both of my parents were faithful third-generation Adventists. After a long civil war, in January 1959 Cuba's revolutionary leaders assumed the country's government and destiny. Initially, the primary purpose was to overcome a bloody tyranny bringing livery and prosperity to the island. However, they quickly evolved, establishing a communist ideology and government which still hold power.

One of the significant consequences of this political reality was the consistent and purposeful program of the communist party to expunge the Christian faith from Cuba. Pastors and believers were taken to prison, Christian literature was banned, and Christian schools were closed. Consequently, the government established a public educational system which undermined the Christian faith and enforced the teaching of an atheist ideology. I received my whole education in that system.

In every course, the teachers integrated the communist atheist ideology. The ideas not only undermined the main tenets of the Christian worldview, like God's good creation, the reality of the image of God in humanity, and the salvation in Christ; they also aimed to deconstruct Christian ethical and moral teaching. Like all my Adventist friends, I spent more than eight hours daily listening, learning, and repeating those ideas. Christian education was not an available option. By the grace of God, however, my brother, many of my Adventist friends, and I never rejected our Christian Adventist faith, although we were confronting persecution, mockery, and missing educational opportunities. How could I maintain my Christian faith and practice in that environment? The answer is Christian education at home.

While I needed to attend the schools, my parents, Francisco and Mercedes Fernandez, did not wholly rely on the public school system for my education. They consistently and almost daily checked the content of my school learning. *What did you learn today at school? What did the teacher teach you?* These questions were common in my household while we were growing up. My parents purposely engaged with correcting those schools' ideas, replacing them with the Christian worldview.

For example, in school, the teacher taught me about my evolution from an inferior form of life, but at home, my parents emphasized my origin as a bearer of God's image and likeness. I could intellectually repeat and understand Darwin's views on the origin of species, but I believed in the creation of a loving God. In school, my teachers emphasized finding 'salvation' or the solution to human problems in humanity and the development of science. While science and education have provided significant advances to humanity, they have been unable to solve the problem of human sin, greed, and evil. So, my parents taught me to trust in Christ as the Savior and the only one able to provide a final solution to the crisis in our world. In the schools, the professors continually undermined the biblical principles of sexuality and family. At home, my mom and dad emphasized the principles of healthy Christian sexuality and the principles of founding a Christian family.

I never attended an Adventist school. I never enjoyed the blessings of being educated under a Christian teacher's care. But I received one of the best Adventist educations at home. My parents were not teachers; in reality, they themselves had only completed secondary education. Nonetheless, I owe entirely to them my Christian principles and education. Adventist education is a blessing, and I firmly believe our schools are the best place to send our children. But there is no substitute for a Christian education at home.[2]

One of the things that is important about Abner's story is how he brings out the worldview that the public schools in Cuba attempted to form in the students and what his family did to correct that worldview. As discussed earlier in this book, there are thousands of forces out there on the internet, in shopping malls, on television, etc. which are trying to disciple our students—but one of the most powerful forces is the curriculum in school. This is, once again, why church schools are so important—because we can form a worldview in harmony with what is being taught at church and hopefully in the home.

This also shows the importance of discipling our students in the public schools where the curriculum is typically based on a naturalistic worldview which teaches evolution as fact and many other ideas contrary to Christianity. George Knight brings this out clearly in his article, "Ground Zero in the Great Controversy: The struggle for the minds and hearts of the next generation."

I thank God there are many good Christian teachers, administrators, and staff working in public schools, but the problem is that they cannot rewrite the curriculum from a Christian perspective, nor can they openly pray with students or teach a Bible class. They can, however, become sponsors of Christian clubs which meet before or after school or even at lunchtime, where they can talk about Jesus and pray with students.

Until we can provide enough support and access to make Adventist education available to every Adventist teenager,

---

[2] Knight, George. "Educating for Eternity," Andrews University Press, 2016.

we must have strong public school ministries to take as many of the principles of Christian education to our young people studying in secular institutions as possible! But before we discuss campus clubs, let's start with after-school programs. After-school programs can be successful for any age but here we will focus on elementary school students.

After-School Programs

I have never been part of a thriving after-school program, but I know they exist. Mormons have before- and after-school programs, at least for high schoolers, and I know Catholics have church schools and campus ministries on college campuses as well. The only time I remember being visited by a pastor while I was in college was by a Lutheran campus minister after going to a Lutheran church with a girlfriend. There are also sports after-school programs run by police officers so they can get to know the students in a fun way, and other civic organizations like Boys and Girls Clubs, etc. So it is obviously possible for Adventists to create after-school programs designed to disciple students, as well.

A couple of years ago I piloted an inner-city after-school program in a city near where I live. I partnered with a local Adventist pastor, Claval Hunter, his church members, and some seminary students. I got permission to use the Encounter Bible curriculum on a trial basis because we wanted the central piece of the after-school program to be Bible class. We also found a seminarian who was a fitness coach to do some fit breaks with the kids, and another seminarian who had spent many years as a teacher to teach the Bible portion. In addition to that, we found a seminary student whose wife was finishing up a tutoring program curriculum as part of her master's program, so we had a focus on body, mind, and spirit like we do in our church schools. The students received 20 minutes of each during the one-hour program.

My idea was to invite kids from the inner-city projects where pastor Hunter and his members spent one Sabbath per month ministering in a primarily African-American community. My wife and I joined in for more than a year in these outreaches and really developed a love for the church and its community.

In addition to inviting kids from the projects, we wanted to invite young people from the church who did not have access to Christian education. This would be a combination of evangelistic outreach to the community, and discipleship for the children of the church. The problem is that our planned start date was interrupted by the Covid-19 pandemic. Everything went online, so we tried Zoom, but it was just too hard to get the kids from the neighborhood to remember to get online at the right time. The original plan was to show up in their neighborhood in a community center. We did get a few church kids involved and helped them with reading, writing, Bible, and fitness, but it was not all we had hoped.

In the meantime, pastor Hunter and his congregation sold their church building and are now in the final phase of purchasing a building in a great location where it can be a center of influence offering programs all week long as well as Sabbath services. We are planning to restart the after-school program once their community center is ready. Maybe some of you will give it a try as well and can give us some tips!

Public High School Visitation

Public school ministries can be run by any pastor or chaplain, and I've always wished that every academy had a dedicated Bible teacher/chaplain who also ran campus ministries at the public high schools. That's essentially what I did as a youth pastor, and I also had a ministry presence at the local community college when one was nearby. I believe it's important to follow kids from campus-to-campus, spending time with them, helping them apply faith to life as they grow in their discipling journey. Even if you cannot run clubs, visiting students at school to share lunch regularly can be a great way to disciple as well.

For simple public high school student visitation, all you have to do is talk to the kids from your church who attend public school and tell them you'd like to stop by and have lunch with them sometime. Tell them you'll bring pizza or tacos or whatever they like, and they can invite a couple of friends to come with them. Just tell them you would like to see their world and talk about what it's like to be a Christian on a public campus. When a student agrees, make sure to talk to their parents to see if it's okay with them (I've never had a parent say no). Then, you simply stop by the school office and let them know you'd like to visit a student at lunchtime. In my case, they called it "counseling" and were very happy to have me on campus at the high school right across the street from my church. They said they simply needed to have a parent call the school letting them know you have their permission. It's that simple!

That's how my campus ministry got started; it was so easy. From there, I dropped in to visit the existing Christian Club and got to know the sponsor after I was finished having lunch with the kids I knew. To make a long story short, I was such a regular on campus that the front office staff paid for me to get a background check and get fully registered as a campus volunteer. Eventually I ended up taking over and running the campus Christian Club, and hosted weeks of prayer right on campus, as well as other various forms of outreach ministry.

I'll give you an overview here of some of the activities you can use to engage with students on campus, but first I'd like to share the story of a youth pastor I worked with when I was still in youth ministry that shows the importance of simply visiting kids at their school. At the time this story was told to me I was filming testimonies for my public high school ministry resource center called Living It. The video is long gone but here is part of the story he told:

JASON

> When I started high school, my family was amazing. I had great parents and a fun brother. We had a trampoline and a swimming pool and everything a kid could want. We were living the dream, having so much fun. We were all involved in church and loved God. Then everything changed.
>
> My parents' marriage was on the rocks and then they got divorced. Everything broke down. We even stopped going to church—my parents just didn't care anymore. In the midst of the chaos, I found myself in public high school instead of academy. I didn't know how God could let this happen and I didn't know what place he had in my life anymore.
>
> Then, one day, my youth pastor said he wanted to come see me at school. I thought, "What? Why would he want to come see me here at my public school?" But I said, "Yeah, that's cool." And he came

to see me, and he said, "You want to go to Taco Bell?" I said, "Taco Bell, yes—I love Taco Bell!" (I still love Taco Bell!) So we went and ate, and he asked me how I was doing, and we talked and he prayed with me.

That made such a huge difference in my life. With my youth pastor's help and encouragement, over time, I decided I still wanted to give my life to God. I'm a youth pastor today partly because of his influence.

Now, as a youth pastor, I want to go see kids at their school just like my pastor came to see me. I want to be there for kids, too. It's so rewarding when you can help someone through a crisis; I really love just being there for kids when they need me.

This youth pastor's story is heartbreaking, but what an amazing turnaround, simply because his youth pastor took the time to visit!

This also reminds me of my own experience. When I went to public high school after graduating from my loving little Adventist elementary school, it was quite a shock for me, too. All my friends went off to boarding academy and I was left alone in a strange new place. Drinking, dances, Friday night football—I was confused too, but no one came to visit me.

After my parents divorced when I was in 7th grade, my dad moved out of state and my mom stopped going to church. I went from being with my church family in everything, all my life through 8th grade, to nothing but getting dropped off at church by myself, with no contact from anyone at church all week long, with no one my age and nothing to do after listening to the sermon.

From my own personal experience, it's easy for me to see why we lose so many public school kids from church.

Christian Club Activities

From this simple beginning of public school visitation you can see the potential is huge. Eventually, I was asked to take over the Christian Club at the public school across the street from my church where I was visiting kids weekly. When you have club status, the club can hold official club events on campus—all student-run with adult advisors. When this happened, the doors opened wide for discipleship and evangelism. Here are a sampling of some of the events we held.

Check-in Time and Devotions

For the first year of my first Christian Club, our main focus was check-in time and taking prayer requests so we could develop personal connections within the group. This worked extremely well while we were all getting to know each other for the first school year. Our focus was sharing how our weeks were going and how we could support each other. Then there would be a student-led devotional I would help kids get ideas for. This is the heart of community-building.

Pizza and Prayer Evangelism

For this activity I would buy 20 pizzas and have my students walk around the campus at lunchtime offering free slices of pizza in return for prayer requests. They went two-by-two, one holding the box of pizza and the other writing requests on a pad of paper. The first time my club did this we received nearly 100 serious requests!

See You at the Pole[3]

See You at the Pole is a national event that takes place on the fourth Wednesday of September every year. Students meet around the flagpole outside their school 30 minutes before school starts to pray for fellow students and teachers, their school, and the country. This is a great time to meet other Christian students and faculty who could be potential Christian Club sponsors.

Campus Beautification

Have your club adopt a planter or some area of campus they will beautify and maintain for all students to enjoy. Alternatively, your club can volunteer with your city's local parks and recreation department to help clean up other planters and parks around town. Any type of community service activity helps draw your club members together and lets the world around you know that you care about helping others just like Jesus did.

Host a Week of Spiritual Emphasis

If you have official club status at your school, you should be allowed to have events with special guest speakers. Have students pass out invitations the week before and get

---

[3] For more information visit https://syatp.com/

permission early-on to use the school theater. Offer free food and have students or leaders share testimonies each day during lunch. You may even be able to bring in a praise band—you don't know until you ask! Cap the week off with a Friday night youth rally at a local church.

Prayer Walk

Walk around your campus by twos before/after school or during lunch and pray for different groups of individuals. Pray for the administrators and secretaries at your school so that they can have a good day and lead the school in a positive way. Thank God they have allowed you to live your faith at school. Pray for the teachers, thanking God for the Christian teachers and praying for them to live their faith at school as well. Also, pray for the non-Christian teachers and ask God to help you be a good witness to them. Pray that the Holy Spirit's presence will be felt on your campus and that students will be kind to each other. Pray that the Christian students will stand strong for their faith and that the non-Christian students will be open to your outreach efforts on their behalf.

I have such great memories of these exciting times on campus; they were some of the best times in my ministry. We also did some sidewalk evangelism where I would teach academy kids how to give a simple survey and then get into Finally, here are a couple more stories just to illustrate how students can take a stand for their faith on campus and how others could really use support while going through great crises with little or no faith-based support.

ABIGAIL

I was born on the beautiful island of Nassau, Bahamas. At the age of three, I immigrated to Jamaica and resided in the parish of Clarendon where I would spend my teenage and early adult life.

From as early as I can remember, I have been a church girl. I was raised like an only child as I was the only one at home for most of my life. My brother was always at his friend's house and many times came home after I was asleep. Therefore, from my earliest years, I was the only child at home and was always in my mother's company. When my mother's friends would visit, I would sit and listen to them speak. I always found comfort in the company of adults and this impacted the way I viewed life and my reasoning abilities.

Maybe this was the reason I was a misfit among my peers. I was called a "granny" and told on many occasions how ugly I was. I began to believe some of these utterances, and I chose to confide in God with all my questions and challenges. He was my best friend; I really didn't have anyone else. He was my go-to on dark and lonely days, primarily during my primary and high school years. I would pray small prayers and I always saw results.

Because I knew God was real, I would spend time with him each day during my childhood and teenage years. All my classmates at the local elementary and middle school in my community knew I was a baptized Christian, hence they held me to a higher standard. This prepared me for high school; I had no reservations about sharing my faith. During the course of the week, I would study my weekly Sabbath School lessons and share my faith with my classmates. My classmates and I would have vibrant discussions about the Sabbath and drinking alcoholic beverages and eating pork. Everyone knew I was a Christian, and I was not ashamed.

OLIVER

My parents became Christian (Seventh-day Adventist) when I was only three years old. I basically grew up as if I were an Adventist all my life. Growing up in Alaska, I was very sheltered. All throughout elementary and middle school, I found myself within the context of the Adventist community. It wasn't until I got into public high school that I started to become more exposed to things of "this world." So many of my peers were into smoking and drinking at an illegal age; it was considered the cool thing to do. I always had a curiosity to join in, but due to my strict Adventist parents and upbringing, it never was possible.

Another thing that created dissatisfaction with my life was that all the "fun" events and things my friends would do were on Saturdays. When I got into college, this really made me feel like I had missed out on so much. Everyone else drank and smoked before graduating. I didn't. Everyone else went to parties and "hooked up" with girls. I didn't. I would say this was the beginning of my dissatisfaction with the life I had. I wanted to experience the things my peers experienced because it seemed that their life was so much better and worth living.

Naturally, when I started college and started to have more freedom and autonomy (I moved out of my parents' home as soon as I graduated), I explored everything I had missed. I attended parties, got drunk, and smoked my lungs out. All of this happened while I was still actively helping my church up in Alaska. They didn't have a leader for the English-speaking congregation (I attended a Korean church) so I naturally stepped up into that position.

I felt a huge disconnect in what I was doing throughout the week and what I was doing at church on the weekends. The more I dug into this lifestyle, the more I realized I wasn't happy. I was searching for some kind of satisfaction and happiness but instead I started to find myself in a dark place of suicidal thoughts and depression. I started to hear from these friends that they, too, were in a dark place, looking for something more.

Around my third year of college, a pastor came to visit Alaska from New York. I had written an article about our church group, and when he saw it, he wanted to visit. I remember picking him up from the airport and having long conversations with him about his career and his mission as a pastor. I didn't grow up with an older brother and wasn't as close to my father during this time, so having someone to look up to was something I really wanted.

The more I talked with him, the more I realized that he went through very similar experiences to mine. Yet it was when he dedicated his life and work to Jesus that he started to find peace and satisfaction. It was at that point he encouraged me to go on a long-term mission trip. At first, I was hesitant because I had never considered going away from home for so long; even more I had never really considered giving up that much time in my life for God. This part of my life was when I slowly started to be exposed to the lives of those who truly lived out what they believed and had fully experienced that satisfaction from God. It was also when I decided to take initiative and go on a mission trip, so that I could experience God for myself.

That year-long mission trip was probably the best thing that could have happened for the trajectory of my life, as I had much more time to spend with God through reading the Bible, praying, and studying. What makes this even better is that by being in a position of leadership, God was able to use my own experience to better connect and communicate with the students. As I looked up to different leaders and others who were so dedicated to living a life for God, I naturally emulated that in my own life. By leading, I was able to share my story of struggle and the victory of finding peace and satisfaction by following Jesus.

I think this was a huge push in a new direction for me. What's even better is that it was this mission trip that built a foundation which would carry me, even to this day. Whenever I meet young people now, I realize that the struggle is essentially the same. There is a search for happiness and satisfaction; the world advertises it one way, and after they pursue that way, they discover it isn't as good as they thought.

My experience may differ due to the age difference, but the principle of finding peace and happiness in a life with Jesus remains. I've been able to take my journey and use it to disciple others into a relationship with Jesus.

My prayer is that more youth pastors and academy chaplains will become more involved in reaching out to ALL high school-aged youth no matter where they are able to attend school. Public school campuses are about far more than even ministering to our own youth. My Christian clubs were mostly non-Adventist kids; it's where you can partner with public school kids from your church to do campus evangelism in many ways. In this setting you can engage in many ministries described in the book *Steps to Christ*:

> In describing his earthly mission, Jesus said, The Lord "has anointed me to preach the gospel to the poor; he has sent me to heal the brokenhearted, to proclaim liberty to the captives and recovery of sight to the blind, to set at liberty those who are oppressed" (Luke 4:18). This was his work. He went around doing good and healing all that were oppressed by Satan… His work gave evidence of his divine anointing. Love, mercy, and compassion were revealed in every act of his life; his heart went out in tender sympathy to the children of men (p. 11-12).

Activity for This Chapter

With these options to engage public high school age youth with, list some of the activities that you resonated with and feel like you could own and make your own. Perhaps, after reading through these activities, new ones have come to your mind, or you are remembering activities you experienced that resonated with you as a youth. Write them down and then see how you can get involved with these activities. Follow up with your local public school, and see how you can start volunteering and being present with the students.

Chapter 12

Helping Live Your Story to the Fullest

Pastors preach from the pulpit and teachers teach from the books—but where the rubber hits the road in discipling children is during the in-between times as we walk together along the way, according to the grand tradition of the Shema. Whether it's between classes, on the playground, after school, on a church campout, or a mission trip; this is where young people really get to know you, and it has been said that "there is no significant learning without a significant relationship."[1] It doesn't matter if the one discipling is a pastor, teacher, or parent—discipling only happens through relationships as we have seen in the dozens of stories in the pages of this book. If these relationships and times together in the real world are missing, our children will have a more difficult time understanding how faith applies to the real-world life they live when no one is looking. I think we often underestimate the power of the simple moments throughout the day.

After my students finished writing and turning in their "Who discipled you?" essays, I told them about a new book I was reading called, "Abuelita Faith (grandma faith): What Women on the Margins Teach Us about Wisdom, Persistence, and Strength." In this book, Kat Armas, a

---

[1] Quote from the Blueprint movie on Adventist Education by Martin Doblmeier.

Cuban-American woman, talks about the often-overlooked influence of women in forming the spiritual lives of young people. She says, "For years I overlooked this detail because I hadn't been trained to recognize the importance or value of women in the Bible."[2] She also says that "theology cannot be divorced from personal story. Story is what connects theory with reality, what gives life to our religious understandings."[3]

She goes on to talk about the how Martin Luther King Jr.'s grandmother was a strong spiritual force in his life, and on the two occasions when he thought she had died, he tried to commit suicide. Armas states, "Imagine where our society would be" without the influence of MLK's grandmother on his life. She goes on to talk about how Howard Thurman was raised by his grandmother and the powerful influence she was on him becoming a great civil rights leader as well.[4]

After reading the first few chapters of "Abuelita Faith," I thought back to my childhood and remembered that my grandmother was the spiritual leader of my family. She was always the one consistently leading out with family devotions whenever I was at her home. She told me how she prayed for God to make a way for me to go to Adventist academy rather than public high school, and when that way opened, she gave me a new set of the "Conflict of the Ages" series of books written by E. G. White. It was the central book in that series, "The Desire of Ages," that I picked up after God gave me the vision in the night that he was calling me out of my college partier life to come and work for him. In the preface of that book I read:

> In the hearts of all mankind, of whatever race or station in life, there are inexpressible longings for

---

[2] Armas, Kat. "Abuelita Faith, What Women on the Margins Teach Us about Wisdom, Persistence, and Strength," Brazos Press, 2021, p. 34.
[3] Armas, p. 26
[4] Armas p. 31

something they do not now possess. This longing is implanted in the very constitution of man by a merciful God, that man may not be satisfied with his present conditions or attainments, whether bad, or good, or better. God desires that the human shall seek the best, and find it to the eternal blessing of his soul.[5]

Satan, by wily scheme and craft, has perverted these longings of the human heart. He makes men believe that this desire may be satisfied by pleasure, by wealth, by ease, by fame, by power; but those who have been thus deceived by him (and they number myriads) find all these things pall upon the sense, leaving the soul as barren and unsatisfied as before. It is God's design that this longing of the human heart should lead to the One who alone is able to satisfy it. The desire is of him that it may lead to him, the fullness and fulfillment of that desire. That fullness is found in Jesus the Christ, the Son of the Eternal God.[6]

Just like James K.A. Smith asks: "What do you want?" White states that Jesus is the one we want—the only one who can fulfill all our needs and desires—this is why he alone is the Desire of all ages. All this made me wonder if it was really my grandmother's fervent prayers on my behalf which moved the hand of God to give me that vision in the night to pick up that book that initiated my journey with Him. I'm sure she knew I was searching and didn't know what I wanted—that I was confused by the world.

I also thought about my church-school teacher at my little one-room school in Minnesota, Mrs. Bimberg. Every morning at school, we started the day with worship. She

---

[5] White, Ellen. "The Desire of Ages," Pacific Press Publishing Association, 1898, p. 17.
[6] White, p. 17.

taught me to love the hymns "In the Garden," "The Old Rugged Cross," "Redeemed," and many others. She taught me scripture and showed a kind, gentle, and loving spirit.

Reading Armas' book helped me realize that Mrs. Bimberg and my grandmother are two of the people who discipled me the most as a child. When I told my students this story and shared some thoughts from this book, many students' hands shot up asking to re-write their "Who discipled you?" essays because they too had overlooked the women who were spiritual leaders in their lives. I hope you spend some time thinking about this as well.

Spiritual foundations are best laid in the lives of children in the elementary school years. They need to be nurtured to know how to feed themselves spiritually and devotionally by the time they graduate from high school and leave their places of spiritual nurture to engage in the young adult journey of self-discovery and making their own lives. From my experience, pastors, teachers, and parents, both women and men, teaming up together, can form the most powerful discipling community young people can experience. As Armas says, "We need one another because no one person or one group of people can fully bear all that is God's image. Instead, each culture, people, or group offers a glimpse of a different aspect of the full image of God."[7]

My prayer is that we can all come together for our children and disciple them according to the great tradition of the Shema, laying a spiritual foundation and filling it with memories of being discipled by people who were full and overflowing with the love of Jesus and the fruits of the Spirit. I believe this is the strongest foundation possible for helping the faith of our children to endure the trials and challenges of life on planet Earth. This is the only

[7] Armas, p. 28

foundation which can see them through to an eternity of peace and happiness with Jesus and all our community of faith in the earth made new.

Finally, I would like to challenge you to keep pressing forward in your own discipleship journey. Get together as pastors, teachers, and parents to discuss the discipleship journey of your church and school and how it is or is not impacting the students and families within your sphere of influence. I highly recommend the Abide Spiritual Master Plan document available at www.adventisteducators.org/2020/12/abide/. Sit down together with your team and get started planning how to do even better than you already are in discipling students to Jesus and journeying with them along the way.

> We proclaim to you the one who existed from the beginning,[a] whom we have heard and seen. We saw him with our own eyes and touched him with our own hands. He is the Word of life. [2] This one who is life itself was revealed to us, and we have seen him. And now we testify and proclaim to you that he is the one who is eternal life. He was with the Father, and then he was revealed to us.[3] We proclaim to you what we ourselves have actually seen and heard so that you may have fellowship with us. And our fellowship is with the Father and with his Son, Jesus Christ.[4] We are writing these things so that you may fully share our joy[b] (1 John 1: 1-4).

Appendices

Appendix A

LOVE LANGUAGES, LEARNING STYLES, AND PERSONALITY TYPES

Each of us have a unique set of learning styles, personalities, and love languages. While there are many resources that may help you discover your unique set, there are a few resources that I would like to recommend. These are not a limited list but can help you get started on your own discovery journey.

- **Learning Styles.** This resource discovers how you learn best: through auditory, visual, kinesthetic, and/or tactile means. The website will lead you to a PDF where you will calculate the total number for each of these four areas to see which ones are your preferred means of learning. https://sarconline.sdes.ucf.edu/wp-content/uploads/sites/19/2017/07/Barsch_Learning_Styles_Inventory11.pdf

- **Temperaments.** The idea of temperaments originates with the ancient Greeks, describing the four main types of human behavior: sanguine, choleric, melancholic, and/or phlegmatic. The website provides 24 statements which you will rate using a five-point scale. It will then calculate your percentage for each temperament. https://openpsychometrics.org/tests/O4TS/

- **Myers-Briggs 16 Personalities.** This personality survey has been used throughout the recent years to help further specify the above four temperament options. Each temperament now has additional layers which may be discovered through this website: https://www.16personalities.com/.

- **Love Language.** Best known because of the work of Gary Chapman, I recommend you take this quiz to uncover your love language. Along with the website quiz, I would encourage you to acquire the book resource that explains the five love languages in detail and how to use the information you learn with knowing your love language(s). The five love languages are words of affirmation, quality time, gifts, acts of service, or physical touch. https://5lovelanguages.com/quizzes/love-language

Appendix B
NOTES ON TEENAGE DEVELOPMENTAL ISSUES BY DON KEELE, JR.

Students moving into this phase of their development would often have them distancing themselves from their parents as a God-given instinct to prepare them to do life apart from their parents. But this move away means it is all the more important they have others in their lives who can continue to point them to Jesus.

Another key characteristic of this stage of life is that young people are moving from concrete operational thinking skills into abstract operational thinking skills. Up to this point in their lives, God has only been seen in the context of how the authority figures in their lives treated them. If they have good parents (or teachers or pastors), they have a good God. If they don't have good parents/teachers/pastors, many view God as abusive or tyrannical.

This shift in thinking skills from concrete to abstract is ever-expanding as they move through their teens and into their 20s, and has massive implications on how they self-ideate and define themselves into adulthood. Teens often look more to peers or societal norms than to their parents in piecing together their own identity, trying on various personas in search of who they are as well as the ultimate meaning of their lives.

Also, because of expanding abilities to understand abstract thought, their relationships are not so clear-cut black and white. Abstract thought allows young people to begin to see nuance in those relationships, and even to begin to apply (often wrongly) motives for why people did something. Once assumed motives are in place, they often act on those assumptions, which further muddies the relational waters.

This is why discipleship to this age group is so important. A caring adult who is spiritually plugged in can come alongside and help steer them into a meaningful relationship with Christ and help them find identity and purpose.

As to resources, here are a few I like—some old, some new. But since Gen Z is different from any previous generation, I think there needs to be a continuum of education, because today's teens are very different from the teens of just eight to ten years ago. Here then, set in a continuum rationale, is what I would suggest.

Besides the fact that we tend to hurry kids through to adulthood ("The Hurried Child" by David Elkind) and they end up experiencing all many things in elementary school we would traditionally have liked to introduce them to during the regular rites of passage in their teens ("All Grown up and No Place to Go" by David Elkind), they grow bored with it all. For example, an international choir tour that used to happen in college now happens in high school, and the regional one that used to happen in high school now happens in elementary. So by the time they get to college, unless the college chorale is doing a world tour, they look at it as a "been-there-done-that." This is true in almost every area of school curricula now.

Young people's constant search for knowledge leads them to believe that to Google something means they have knowledge of it, but it leaves them with very little experience. ("Artificial Maturity" by Tim Elmore). There is also a deep sense of abandonment among teens ("Hurt" by Chap Clark).

Gen Z approaches life totally different than any other Generation ("Meet Gen Z" by James Emery White) and they have more and more to say ("Generation Z Unfiltered" by Tim Elmore). Much research has been done on them ("Gen Z: The Culture, Beliefs and Motivations Shaping the Next Generation" by The Barna Group), and one of the best resources ("Faith For Exiles: 5 Ways for a New Generation to Follow Jesus in Digital Babylon" by Aly Hawkins, David Kinnaman, and Mark Matlock) takes a look at the youth and young adults who stayed in the church and how they were able to build resilience into their faith.

Appendix C
ENCOUNTER: LORDSHIP MODEL AND TRANSFORMATIONAL PLANNING

Framework

The Encounter Bible Curriculum is the newest Bible curriculum for the Seventh-day Adventist school system. While the Encounter website provides ample detail about its curriculum, I would like to include the following visual depiction. It demonstrates the framework for the curriculum: where teachers and students partner together in the learning process. This partnership and collaboration are what I would like to encourage between the church, school, and home spheres. The encounter website is https://encounter.adventisteducation.org/index.html.

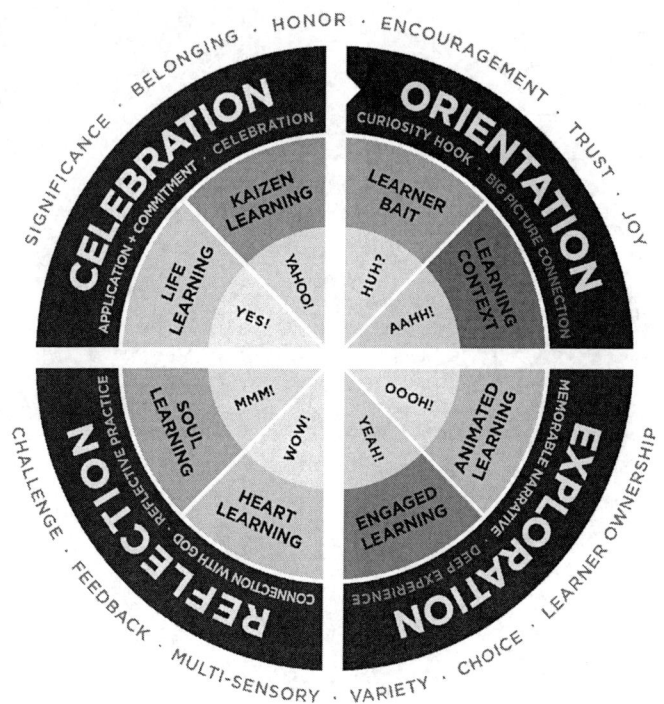